Title I

Unlocking Career Opportunities:

The Power of Soft Skills in Job Searching

King Lain Ozick

Copyright Page

Copyright © 2003 [Your Name]

All rights reserved. No part of this publication may be reproduced, distributed, or transmitted in any form or by any means, including photocopying, recording, or other electronic or mechanical methods, without the prior written permission of the author, except in the case of brief quotations embodied in critical reviews and certain other noncommercial uses permitted by copyright law.

Unauthorized use, reproduction, or distribution of this publication may result in civil and criminal penalties. While every precaution has been taken in the preparation of this publication, the publisher and author assume no responsibility for errors or omissions, or for damages resulting from the use of the information contained herein.

This publication is intended to provide general information and guidance on the subject matter covered. It is not intended to serve as professional advice or replace individual consultation. Readers are advised to consult with a qualified professional before making any decisions or taking any actions based on the information provided in this publication.

The trademarks, logos, and service marks mentioned in this publication are the property of their respective owners and are used for identification purposes only. Such use does not imply any affiliation with or endorsement by the owners of these trademarks, logos, and service marks.

ISBN: 9798852367686

Cover design by Israel Okundaye

Quote Page

"Job searching is not just about submitting applications and waiting for a response. It's about taking control of your career destiny and proactively creating opportunities. By leveraging your unique strengths and effectively communicating your value proposition, you can navigate the job market with confidence and unlock a world of possibilities." - Martin Yates, Author of "Knock 'Em Dead Job Search Strategies".

About the Author

The author of the new release "Unlocking Career Opportunities: The Power of Soft Skills in Job Searching" is a renowned expert in the field of career development and job search strategies. With years of experience and a deep understanding of the job market, this author has helped countless individuals achieve success in their careers.

Known for his insightful and practical approach, the author emphasizes the importance of soft skills in job searching. He believe that while technical qualifications and experience are essential, it is the mastery of soft skills that truly sets job seekers apart and opens doors to new opportunities.

Through this book, the author provides valuable guidance on how to effectively showcase and leverage soft skills during the job search process. He offers practical tips, real-life examples, and actionable strategies to help readers improve their self-presentation, networking, and communication skills.

"Unlocking Career Opportunities: The Power of Soft Skills in Job Searching" is a comprehensive resource that empowers job seekers to take control of their career paths and maximize their potential in today's competitive job market.

Included in his collection is a book about caring for elderly parents. "Aging Parents: How to take care of parents when they are old."
https://a.co/d/cno4v93

Table of Content

Title Page 1

Copyright Page 2

Quote Page 4

About the Author 5

Introduction 9

Communication skills 32

Teamwork - Unlock Career Potential through Collaboration 52

Time Management 72

Adaptability: Accepting Change and Succeeding in the Labor Market 101

Unleash Your Leadership Potential: a Guide for Job Seekers 117

Understanding the Purpose and Types of Behavioral Questions 129

Conclusion 171

Recap of Key Points 174

Acknowledgement 180

Bonus - Unlock achievements Job interview Jargons to Avoid 184

Introduction

If you're a jobseeker, you know that getting a job is not just about having the right qualifications. Hiring managers and recruitment agencies search for candidates with the right soft skills, such as communication, teamwork, problem-solving, and time management. These skills are essential for success in any workplace, and without them, your chances of getting hired are significantly reduced.

That's where "Unlocking Career Opportunities: The Power of Soft Skills in Job Searching" comes in.

This book is a must-read for anyone who wants to strengthen their soft skills and ace their interviews.

Written by King Lain Ozick with contributions from experienced recruiters and human resources professionals, this book provides a comprehensive guide to developing the soft skills that are in high demand. It includes practical tips and advice on how to improve your communication, teamwork, problem-solving, and time management skills, as well as how to prepare for and ace behavioral-based interview questions.

This book is not just for jobseekers, however. It's also an invaluable resource for human resources professionals and hiring managers who want to identify and recruit candidates with the right skills. It provides insights into the hiring process, including how to craft effective job descriptions, screen resumes, conduct interviews, and make hiring decisions based on soft skill assessments.

Overall, "Unlocking Career Opportunities: The Power of Soft Skills in Job Searching" is a must-have for anyone who wants to excel in their career. Whether you're a jobseeker, a human resource professional, or a hiring manager, this book will help you develop the soft skills that are essential for success in the workplace.

Why Soft Skills Are Important for Job Seekers

In today's job market, employers are not just looking for specialized skills. They want candidates who possess strong soft skills, which are personal attributes and interpersonal skills that enable individuals to interact effectively with others.

Soft skills are the abilities to communicate well, work in a team, solve problems, adapt to changes, manage time effectively, and lead others. Unlike technical skills that are specific to a job or industry, communication skills can be transferred between roles and industries.

Why Are Soft Skills Important?

Soft skills are important for several reasons:

1. Building Relationships

In any workplace, building relationships with colleagues, customers, and stakeholders is essential for success. Soft skills like communication, teamwork, and empathy are critical for building trust and rapport with others, and for resolving conflicts and misunderstandings. Without these skills, it can be difficult to build strong working relationships, which can ultimately impact your ability to succeed in your role.

2. Effective Leadership

Leadership is not just about technical expertise – it's also about the ability to inspire and motivate others. Soft skills like communication, empathy, and teamwork are essential for effective leadership, as they enable leaders to build strong relationships with their team members, understand their needs and motivations, and create a conducive and productive working environment.

3. Highly Valued by Employers

Employers are increasingly aware of the value of social skills in the workplace. In fact, a recent survey by LinkedIn found that 57% of leaders say soft skills are more important than hard skills. This is because soft skills are essential for building strong teams, fostering innovation, and driving business success.

4. Standing Out from the Competition

In a competitive job market, having strong soft skills can help you stand out from other candidates. Employers are tracking down candidates who not only have the technical skills to do the job, but also the interpersonal skills to work effectively with others and contribute to the overall success of the organization.

How to Develop Soft Skills

So, how can you develop and demonstrate your soft skills as a jobseeker? Here are some tips:

1. Practice Active Listening

Active listening is an essential soft skill that involves fully concentrating on what someone is saying, understanding their message, and responding appropriately. To practice active listening, make eye contact, ask clarifying questions, and avoid interrupting or judging the speaker.

2. Join a Team or Volunteer

Joining a team, volunteering is a great way to develop your teamwork skills and build relationships with others. Seek opportunities to join a sports team, community group, or volunteer organization, and focus on collaborating effectively with others to achieve common goals.

3. Seek Feedback and Take Criticism Gracefully

Seeking feedback and taking criticism gracefully are important soft skills that demonstrate your willingness to learn and grow. Ask for feedback from colleagues, mentors, or supervisors, and be open to constructive criticism. Use feedback as an opportunity to improve your skills and performance.

4. Practice Time Management

Time management is a critical soft skill that involves prioritizing tasks, setting goals, and managing your time effectively to meet deadlines. To elevate your time management skills, create a schedule or to-do list, prioritize your tasks, and avoid procrastination.

5. Develop Your Communication Skills

Effective communication is a key soft skill that involves expressing yourself clearly and listening actively to others. To expand your communication skills, practice speaking clearly and concisely, use nonverbal cues like body language and tone of voice, and ask for feedback on your communication style.

6. Stay Positive and Adaptable

Staying positive and adaptable is an indispensable soft skill that demonstrates your ability to handle change and uncertainty. To develop this skill, focus on staying optimistic in the face of challenges, be flexible and open to new ideas, and take initiative to solve problems.

7. Emotional Intelligence

Emotional intelligence is the ability to recognize and manage your emotions, as well as the emotions of others. It involves being self-aware, empathetic, and socially skilled. Emotional intelligence is an essential soft skill that can help you build strong relationships, resolve conflicts, and lead effectively. To develop your emotional intelligence, practice self-reflection, empathy, and active listening.

8. Critical Thinking

Critical thinking involves interpreting information, evaluating arguments, and solving issues. It's a critical soft skill that can help you make informed decisions, identify opportunities for improvement, and innovate. To develop your critical thinking skills, practice asking questions, consider multiple perspectives, and challenging assumptions.

Soft skills are essential for success in today's job market. They enable individuals to build strong relationships, demonstrate effective leadership skills, and stand out from the competition. By developing and demonstrating your soft skills, you can increase your chances of landing your dream job and achieving long-term career success. So, take the time to develop your soft skills, and you'll be well on your way to a successful career.

The Role of Soft Skills in Business and Money: A Comprehensive Guide

In today's fast-paced business world, soft skills are becoming increasingly important. While hard skills are essential, it is often the soft skills that make the difference between success and failure. Soft skills are traits that help people interact effectively with others. These include the essential skills encompassed in this list which are communication, working effectively in a team, finding solutions to problems, being adaptable and managing time efficiently. In this guide, we will explore the role of soft skills in business and money, and how they can help jobseekers, employers, and firms succeed.

Recruitment

Recruiters are increasingly prioritizing soft skills when hiring new employees. In fact, a LinkedIn survey found that 92% of recruiters and hiring managers agree that soft skills are just as important as professional skills. This is because soft skills are essential for building relationships with colleagues, clients, and customers. They also enable employees to work effectively in teams, handle conflicts, and manage their time efficiently.

Jobseekers that possess strong soft skills are more likely to be successful in the recruitment process. This is because recruiters are searching for individuals who can adapt to changing situations, communicate effectively, and work collaboratively. Soft skills are also essential for leadership positions, as they enable individuals to motivate and inspire their teams.

Human Resource

Human resource departments play a critical role in identifying and developing soft skills in employees. They are responsible for creating training programs that help employees develop these skills. HR departments also provide feedback and coaching to employees to help them strengthen their soft skills.

Firms that invest in developing their employees' soft skills benefit from increased productivity, higher employee engagement, and improved customer satisfaction. Employees who possess strong soft skills are also more likely to stay with the company and advance their careers.

Undergraduates

Undergraduates who are preparing to enter the workforce need to develop their soft skills to increase their chances of getting hired. In fact, a study by the National Association of Colleges and Employers found that 80% of employers are looking for graduates with strong soft skills.

Undergraduates can develop their soft skills through internships, extracurricular activities, and part-time jobs. These experiences provide opportunities to develop communication, teamwork, and time management skills. Undergraduates can also take courses in leadership, public speaking, and conflict resolution to develop their soft skills.

Job Research

Job research is an essential part of the job search process. Jobseekers need to research the company and the job they are applying for to understand the skills and qualities the employer is looking for. This research can help jobseekers tailor their resumes and cover letters to highlight their soft skills.

Jobseekers can also prepare for job interviews by practicing their communication and problem-solving skills. They can also prepare examples of how they have demonstrated their soft skills in previous jobs or experiences.

Soft Skills and Business Success

Soft skills play a crucial role in business success. Employees with strong soft skills can help businesses increase their revenue and profits. For instance, effective communication skills can help sales representatives close deals and negotiate contracts. Good time management skills can help employees meet deadlines and increase productivity.

Soft skills also play a role in customer satisfaction. Employees who possess strong soft skills can build strong relationships with customers, leading to repeat business and positive reviews. This, in turn, can increase the company's revenue and reputation.

Furthermore, employees with strong soft skills are more likely to be promoted to leadership positions. This is because leadership positions require individuals who can motivate and inspire their teams, communicate effectively, and handle conflicts. Employees who possess these skills are more likely to be successful in leadership roles, leading to increased revenue and profits for the company.

Soft skills are essential in business and money. They enable employees to communicate effectively, work collaboratively, and handle conflicts, leading to increased productivity, customer satisfaction, and revenue. Employers who prioritize soft skills in their recruitment and training processes are more likely to be successful eventually. Jobseekers that develop their soft skills are more likely to be hired and advance their careers. Soft skills are not only important for individuals but also firms and the economy as a whole. By investing in soft skills' development, businesses can increase their revenue and profits, while also contributing to the overall success of the economy.

How Easy Skills Can Help You Stand Out to Human Resources

Possessing technical knowhow is not enough to secure a job position. Employers are seeking for candidates who possess a combination of technical and soft skills. Soft skills are very important in the workplace. Like we pointed out earlier,

Soft skills are qualities that help people get along well with others. These skills are essential in the workplace, as they help individuals to communicate, collaborate and build relationships with colleagues, clients, and customers. In this article, we will discuss how soft skills can help you stand out to human resources.

Soft skills are very important in the workplace. This is because soft skills are essential in building a positive work environment, improving productivity, and enhancing customer service.

One of the ways that soft skills can help you stand out to human resources is by enhancing your communication skills. Effective communication is crucial in the workplace, as it helps to build relationships, resolve conflicts, and promote teamwork. When you possess excellent communication skills, you can articulate your ideas clearly and concisely, listen actively to others, and express yourself confidently. This makes you an asset to any team, as you can communicate effectively with colleagues, clients, and customers.

Another way that soft skills can help you stand out to human resources is by enhancing your leadership skills. Leadership skills are essential in the workplace, as they enable individuals to inspire, motivate, and guide others. When you possess exceptional leadership skills, you can delegate tasks effectively, provide constructive feedback, and inspire others to achieve their goals. This makes you an asset to any team, as you can lead by example and inspire others to do their best.

In addition to communication and leadership skills, soft skills such as adaptability, creativity, and problem-solving are also highly valued by human resources. Adaptability is the means which people are being able to adjust to new situations as soon as possible. In today's fast-paced work environment, adaptability is essential, as it enables individuals to cope with change and uncertainty. Creativity means thinking in new and different ways to solve problems. This is essential in the workplace, as it enables individuals to find new and better ways of doing things. Problem solving involves the capacity to recognize, assess, and resolve issues. This is essential in the workplace, as it enables individuals to overcome challenges and achieve their goals.

Soft skills are also essential in building relationships with colleagues, clients, and customers. When you possess excellent soft skills, you can build rapport with others, demonstrate empathy, and show respect for others' opinions. This makes you an asset to any team, as you can work effectively with others and build strong relationships with clients and customers.

Possessing soft skills is essential in today's job market. Soft skills such as communication, leadership, adaptability, creativity, and problem-solving are highly valued by human resources. These skills enable individuals to interact effectively with others, build relationships, and achieve their goals. If you want to stand out to human resources, it is essential to develop your soft skills. You can do this by attending training programs, seeking feedback from colleagues, and practicing your skills regularly. By developing your soft skills, you can become an asset to any team and enhance your career prospect.

Leadership Skills:

Leadership skills are essential for any individual who wants to become an effective leader. These skills enable individuals to inspire, motivate, and guide others towards achieving their goals.

Here are some of the most important leadership skills with examples:

1. Communication: Effective communication is crucial in leadership. Leaders must be able to articulate their ideas clearly and concisely, listen actively to others, and express themselves confidently. For example, a leader might use their communication skills to inspire their team to work towards a common goal.

2. Visionary: A leader must have a clear vision of what they want to achieve. This enables them to set goals and develop strategies to achieve them. For example, a leader might have a vision of creating a sustainable business model that benefits both the environment and society.

3. Strategic Thinking: Leaders must be able to think strategically and make decisions based on sound judgment. This involves analyzing data, identifying trends, and anticipating future challenges. For example, a leader might use strategic thinking to develop a long-term plan for their organization.

4. Empathy: Leaders must be able to understand and empathize with the needs and concerns of their team members. This involves showing compassion, being a good listener, and providing support when required. For example, a leader might use empathy to support an employee who is going through a difficult time.

5. Delegation: Leaders must be able to delegate tasks effectively. This means figuring out what each team member is good at and giving them tasks that match their abilities. For example, a leader might delegate a project to a team member who has expertise in that area.

6. Decision-making: Leaders must be able to make decisions quickly and effectively. This involves analyzing data, considering the perspectives of others, and weighing the pros and cons of

different options. For example, a leader might use decision-making skills to choose the best course of action for their organization.

7. Motivation: Leaders must be able to motivate their team members to achieve their goals. This involves recognizing their achievements, providing feedback, and setting challenging but achievable goals. For example, a leader might use motivation to encourage their team to work harder towards achieving a common goal.

8. Coaching: Leaders must be able to coach their team members to help them boost their skills and achieve their goals. This involves providing feedback, setting expectations, and providing guidance when needed. For example, a leader might use coaching skills to help a team member polish their communication skill

9. Conflict Resolution: Leaders must be able to resolve conflicts effectively. This involves listening to both sides, identifying the root cause of the conflict, and finding a solution that satisfies both parties. For example, a leader might use conflict resolution skills to resolve a disagreement between team members.

10. Time Management: Leaders must be able to manage their time effectively to ensure that they can achieve their goals. This involves setting priorities, delegating tasks, and avoiding distractions. For example, a leader might use time management skills to ensure that they can meet deadlines and achieve their goals.

Leadership skills are essential to anyone who wants to become an effective leader. These skills include communication, visionary, strategic thinking, empathy, delegation, decision-making, motivation, coaching, conflict resolution, and time management. By developing these skills, individuals can become successful leaders who can inspire, motivate, and guide their team members towards achieving their goals.

Below is a list of simple skills and technology skills explained in basic terms.

Soft Skills:

1. Communication: The ability to communicate and listen.

2. Collaboration: The ability to work well together with others towards a common goal.

3. Time Management: The ability to prioritize tasks and manage time effectively.

4. Adaptability: The ability to adapt to new situations and cope with change.

5. Problem Solving: The ability to identify and solve problems creatively.

6. Leadership: Leadership means being able to make others feel excited and motivated to work together and reach the same goals.

7. Emotional Intelligence: The ability to understand and manage the emotions of self and others.

8. Creativity: The ability to come up with new and creative ideas.

Technology skills:

1. Programming: The ability to write and understand computer code.

2. Data Analytics: The ability to analyze and interpret data using statistical methods.

3. Website development: The ability to create and maintain websites.

4. Graphic Design: The skill to make pictures and graphics using computer programs.

5. Network Administration: The ability to manage and maintain computer networks.

6. Cybersecurity: The skill to keep computer systems and networks safe from unauthorized entry or harm.

7. Cloud Computing: The ability to manage and maintain systems and services in the cloud.

8. Database Management: The ability to manage and maintain databases.

Communication skills

Effective communication skills are essential for success in both your personal and professional life. Communication is when people or groups share information, thoughts, and ideas with each other. It includes verbal and nonverbal cues such as body language, tone of voice, and facial expressions.

Effective communication can help people build lasting relationships, resolve conflicts, and achieve goals. One of the most important things to do when talking to someone is to listen carefully and show that you are paying attention. Active listening involves paying attention to the speaker, acknowledging their message, and responding accordingly. It is very important to understand the speaker's point of view and show empathy. Active listening can help people build trust, improve relationships, and avoid misunderstandings.

Another important communication skill is assertiveness. Being assertive is expressing your thoughts, feelings, and opinions clearly and confidently, while respecting the rights and feelings of others. It is very important to communicate confidently to avoid misunderstandings, protect yourself and negotiate effectively.

Nonverbal communication is another important aspect of communication skills. Nonverbal cues like facial expressions, body language, and tone of voice can communicate a lot about a person's feelings and intentions. It is very important to be aware of your own nonverbal cues and interpret the nonverbal cues of others to communicate effectively.

Effective communication skills are important in the workplace. Employers value employees who can communicate effectively with colleagues, clients, and customers. Effective communication can increase productivity, build trust, and improve teamwork. It is important to communicate clearly, actively listen and be assertive in the workplace.

In today's digital age, communication skills become even more important. With the rise of remote work and virtual communication, people need to be able to communicate effectively through various digital channels such as email, video conferencing, and instant messaging. It is very important in digital communication to be clear, concise and to use the right tone and language.

Communication skills are also important for job seekers. Effective communication can help job seekers build relationships with potential employers, demonstrate their qualifications, and express interest in the job.

Job seekers need to communicate clearly and confidently during job interviews, networking events, and other interactions with potential employers.

Active listening is an important communication skill for job seekers. During job interviews, job seekers should listen carefully to the interviewer's questions, take note of their message, and respond appropriately. Active listening can help job seekers understand an employer's needs and expectations and tailor their response accordingly.

Persistence is another important communication skill for job seekers. Candidates must be able to confidently demonstrate their qualifications and interest in the job. Confidence can help job seekers stand out from other candidates and demonstrate confidence and enthusiasm for the job.

Nonverbal communication is also important for job seekers. **During interviews, candidates should pay attention to body language, tone of voice, and facial expressions.** Nonverbal cues can convey a lot about a person's confidence, interest, and enthusiasm. Job seekers should use nonverbal cues to effectively communicate and convey their qualifications and interest in the job.

Effective communication skills are the key to success in both your personal and professional life. Communication skills include active listening, persistence, and nonverbal communication. It's important to develop these skills to build lasting relationships, resolve conflicts, and achieve your goals. By improving communication skills, people can optimize their personal and professional lives and increase their chances of career success.

Speaking With Confidence and Clarity

Effective conversation depends not only on what you say, but also on how you say it. Speaking confidently and clearly is an important communication skill that can help people communicate their messages effectively and achieve their goals. In this section, we will discuss how to develop confidence and clear speech and overcome common problems.

One of the most common problems with speaking confidently and clearly is anxiety. Many people feel nervous or anxious when speaking in front of a crowd or in front of other people. However, anxiety can affect your ability to communicate and deliver messages effectively. To overcome anxiety, it's important to exercise and prepare in advance. Practice speaking in front of a mirror or with a friend and prepare your message and main points in advance.

Another problem with speaking confidently and clearly is using the right language and tone. *It is very important to use language that is clear, concise, and appropriate to your audience* and situation. Avoid jargon or technical terms that your audience may not understand.

In addition, tone of voice can convey a lot about a person's confidence and enthusiasm. Use a confident, enthusiastic, and engaging tone of voice.

Nonverbal cues are also important when you speak confidently and clearly. Nonverbal cues, such as body language and facial expressions, can communicate a lot about a person's confidence and enthusiasm. ***Use open and confident body language, such as standing up straight, making eye contact, and using hand gestures correctly.***

In addition, facial expressions can show emotion and enthusiasm. Use facial expressions that match your voice and message. An effective way to develop confidence and speak clearly is to practice public speaking. Public speaking involves speaking in front of a group of people, such as during a presentation or speech. Public speaking can help people develop confidence, improve speaking skills, and overcome anxiety.

Practice speaking in front of a small group of people, such as friends or family members, and gradually grow your audience.

Another way to develop confidence and a clear voice is to get feedback from others. Feedback can help people identify areas for improvement and develop speaking skills. Ask friends, family, or colleagues to rate your speaking skills, such as tone of voice, body language, and clarity.

Speaking confidently and clearly is an important communication skill that can help people communicate their messages effectively and achieve their goals. To develop confidence and clear speech, people must overcome common problems such as anxiety, use appropriate language and tone, and use nonverbal cues effectively.

Additionally, practicing public speaking and giving feedback can help people develop speaking skills and improve their confidence and clarity.

By improving their speaking skills, people can improve their personal and professional lives and increase their chances of career success.

Listening and Understanding Others

Effective communication is not just about speaking, but also about listening and understanding others. The ability to listen and understand others is an important communication skill that can help people build lasting relationships, resolve conflicts, and achieve goals. In this section, we will discuss how to develop listening comprehension skills and overcome common problems.

One of the most common problems with listening and understanding others is distraction. Many people have difficulty focusing on the speaker and may be distracted by other things, such as the phone or their surroundings. To overcome distractions, it is important to be present and mindful. Focus on the speaker, maintain eye contact, and avoid multitasking.

Another problem with listening and understanding others is assumptions. Many people may assume they know what the speaker is trying to say, or may jump to conclusions without fully understanding the message. ***To overcome assumptions, it is important to actively listen and ask questions.*** Clarify the speaker's message and ask for more information if needed.

Nonverbal cues are also important in listening to and understanding others. Nonverbal cues can communicate a lot about a speaker's feelings and intentions. Pay attention to the speaker's nonverbal cues and use them to better understand the message. Also, use appropriate nonverbal cues like nodding or smiling to show that you're listening and interested.

An effective way to develop listening and comprehension skills is to practice active listening. Active listening involves paying attention to the speaker, acknowledging their message, and responding accordingly. It is very important to understand the speaker's point of view and show empathy. Active listening can help people build trust, improve relationships, and avoid misunderstandings.

Another way to develop listening and comprehension skills is to get feedback from others. Feedback can help people identify areas for improvement and develop listening skills. Ask for feedback from a variety of sources on your listening skills such as mindfulness, empathy, and understanding. The ability to listen and understand others is an important communication skill in the workplace. Employers value employees who can actively listen to and understand the views of others. Effective listening can increase productivity, build trust, and improve teamwork. It is very important to actively listen, show empathy, and understand the views of others in the workplace.

Active listening is an important communication skill for career growth. During interviews, candidates should listen carefully to the interviewer's questions, take note of their message, and respond appropriately. Active listening can help job seekers understand an employer's needs and expectations and tailor their response accordingly.

The ability to listen and understand others is an important communication skill that can help people build lasting relationships, resolve conflicts, and achieve goals. To develop listening and comprehension skills, people must overcome common challenges such as distractions and assumptions, use nonverbal cues effectively, and practice active listening. Additionally, seeking feedback and practicing active listening can help people develop listening skills and improve their ability to understand others. By improving listening and comprehension skills, people can improve their personal and professional lives and increase their chances of career success.

In addition to body language and facial expressions, other forms of nonverbal cues include:

1. Eye contact. Eye contact is a powerful nonverbal signal that can convey interest, attention, and confidence.

2. Dumb. Hand gestures can help convey meaning and emphasize meaning in communication. For example, pointing or waving can draw attention to a particular object or person.

3. Outside. Posture can show confidence, authority, and openness. Standing up straight and maintaining an open posture can help convey trust and openness to those around you.

4. Proximity: Close or physical distance can convey different messages in communication. For example, standing too close to someone could be seen as being aggressive or rude, and standing too far away could be seen as disinterested or aloof.

5. Touch. In the process of communication, touch can convey many different emotions and messages. For example, a handshake can show respect and professionalism, while a hug can show warmth and affection.

6. Tone: Tone can convey different emotions and messages in communication. For example, a monotone voice can show boredom or

disinterest, while a lively and enthusiastic voice can show excitement and interest.

7. Appearance. Appearance can also convey many different messages in communication. Professional attire can show respect and professionalism, while casual wear can create a more casual and informal tone.

By recognizing and using nonverbal cues effectively, people can improve their communication skills and deliver messages more effectively.

In addition to friends, family, and colleagues, candidates can get feedback from a variety of sources, such as:

1. Professional networking groups. Joining professional networking groups or attending industry events can provide an opportunity to network with experts in your field and get feedback on your job search strategy.

2. Career Coach. Hiring a career coach can provide job seekers with personalized feedback on their

job search strategies, resumes, cover letters, and interviewing skills.

3. Internet community. Joining online communities like LinkedIn groups or job search forums can give job seekers the opportunity to connect with other job seekers and get feedback on their job search strategies.

4. Former employer. Reaching out to former employers or colleagues can provide job seekers with valuable information about their strengths, weaknesses, and areas for improvement.

5. Recruitment agency. Working with recruitment agencies can provide job seekers with feedback on their job search strategies and help them identify job openings that match their skills and experience.

6. Job search websites. Several job sites offer reviews of resumes and cover letters, as well as tips for improving job search strategies and interviewing skills.

Job seekers can get feedback from a variety of sources, and seeking feedback from multiple sources can provide job seekers with valuable insight into their job search strategy and help them identify potential problems and areas that need improvement.

Job site are an essential tool for job seekers as they provide a centralized platform to access a variety of job opportunities. These sites simplify the job search process by allowing users to search for jobs based on their interests, connect with potential employers, and gather valuable information about Jobs, Company and industry.

Find below some job sites that benefit you in your job search.

1. Indeed (www.indeed.com)

2. LinkedIn (www.linkedin.com)

3. Glassdoor (www.glassdoor.com)

4. CareerBuilder (www.careerbuilder.com)

5. Monster (www.monster.com)

6. Simply Hired (www.simplyhired.com)

7. Zip Recruiter (www.ziprecruiter.com)

8. Craigslist (www.craigslist.org)

9. US Jobs (www.usajobs.gov) - for government jobs in the United States10. Idealist (www.idealist.org) - for nonprofit and social impact jobs.

Written Communication

Written communication is a form of communication that involves the use of written words or texts to convey a message or information. It is a method of expressing thoughts, ideas or instructions in written language. In written communication, messages can be conveyed through many mediums such as letters, emails, memos, reports, articles and even text messages. This allows individuals or organizations to communicate with others who may not be physically present or in real time.

One of the main benefits of written communication is that it provides a permanent record of the communication that you can refer back to at any time. It also allows for careful thought and planning before delivering a message as authors can revise and edit their wording to ensure clarity and accuracy. Written communication is essential in professional environments as it is often used for formal communication in organizations. It helps to communicate important policies, procedures, and information to employees or stakeholders. It is also widely used in academia for research papers, essays or assignments.

Furthermore, written communication allows for effective communication between different cultures and languages. This allows speakers of different languages to communicate through written translations.

However, written communication also has its limitations. The immediate response and nonverbal cues that accompany face-to-face or verbal communication are missing, which can sometimes lead to misunderstandings or misinterpretations. It also requires good reading and writing skills to convey messages effectively and clearly.

Let's turn our searchlight to how written communication can resonate with job hunting.

Written communication is a valuable tool for job seekers for several reasons:

1. CV and cover letter: Job seekers use written communication to create resumes and cover letters. These documents are necessary to introduce job seekers to potential employers and highlight their skills, qualifications and experience. A well-written resume and cover letter can make a good first impression and increase your chances of getting an interview.

2. Application form: Many job applications require applicants to fill out application forms or answer certain questions in writing. Effective written communication skills are essential to delivering clear and concise answers that are relevant to the job.

3. Networking: Written communication is also important for networking during the job search. Job seekers often connect with experts in their field through platforms like LinkedIn or email. Writing well-thought-out messages can help you connect, seek advice, or learn about potential job openings.

4. Email correspondence: E-mail is a common method of communication during the job search process. Job seekers use email to track

applications, schedule interviews, or ask questions. Having strong written communication skills ensures that these emails are professional, clear and effective in conveying the intended message.

5. Thank You Letter: After the interview, it is customary to send a thank you letter or email to express your appreciation and confirm your interest in the position. Well-written thank you letters can leave a positive impression on a hiring manager and demonstrate professionalism and attention to detail.

6. Internet presence. In the digital age, job seekers often have an online presence through platforms like LinkedIn or personal websites.

Overall, written communication is an essential tool for job seekers as it allows them to effectively introduce themselves, communicate their qualifications, and interact with potential employers throughout the job search process. Strong written communication skills can greatly increase a job seeker's chances of landing a job.

Teamwork - Unlock Career Potential through Collaboration

Unity plays an important role in helping people in their careers. In this chapter, we look at the value of teamwork, its benefits, and effective strategies for developing and demonstrating teamwork skills in behavioral interviews.

The Power of Teamwork in Your Career:

Harnessing the power of teamwork is crucial to unlocking your career potential. Employers value candidates who can work effectively with others to achieve set goals.

Benefits of Teamwork in your Career Path:

Teamwork have many benefits that can boost your career, from increasing productivity and efficiency to stimulating creativity and innovation. Learn how effective teamwork can help you stand out in the competitive job market and how teamwork contributes to a positive work environment, leading to greater job satisfaction and long-term career.

Mastering Teamwork Skills in Behavioral Conversations:
During interviews, recruiters often evaluate a candidate's ability to communicate and collaborate effectively with others. By demonstrating strong teamwork skills, job seekers can demonstrate the ability to work well in a team environment.

Teamwork can be of great benefit to job seekers for a variety of reasons.

Here are some examples of how teamwork can benefit candidates, based on actual UK agencies:

1. Job Sharing: In a competitive job market, recruitment agencies like Reed.co.uk or Hays can get a lot of leads. When working in groups, candidates can share relevant job offers with each other. This can increase your chances of finding

suitable roles that may not be found individually.

2. Networking opportunities: Many claims agencies host networking events or job fairs where job seekers can connect with employers and industry professionals. Working as a team, job seekers can attend these events together, exchange contacts and expand their professional network. These joint efforts can lead to more opportunities and recommendations.

3. Check calls and responses. Teamwork allows candidates to conduct face-to-face interviews with each other and give constructive feedback. This practice helps you improve your interviewing skills, boost your confidence, and identify areas for improvement. Agencies like Michael Page or Robert Half often offer interview coaching services for job seekers.

4. Review resumes and cover letters. Job seekers can share and view their resumes and cover letters. This collaborative effort ensures that all documents are well-written, error-free, and appropriate for specific job duties. This can greatly increase your chances of being noticed by agencies like Manpower or Randstad.

5. Share and learn skills: Teamwork allows candidates to share their knowledge and experiences. For example, if a team member is proficient in a particular software or programming language, they can train others to improve the group's overall skill set. This can be helpful when agencies like Adecco or Page Staff are looking for candidates with specific technical skills.

6. Mental support and motivation. Finding a job can be a stressful and unmotivated process. By working as a team, candidates can provide each other with moral support, encouragement, and motivation. This support system can help people stay positive, focused and persistent in their job search even during difficult times.

Teamwork can be of significant benefit to job seekers. By working as a team, job seekers can increase their chances of finding the right position and being employed by recruitment agencies anywhere in the world.

Collaborate Effectively With Others

Mastering soft skills, such as working effectively with others, is critical to career success. This chapter examines the importance of teamwork and offers practical advice on how to be successful in a team environment.

We'll look at cases where collaborating with others can benefit job seekers, using the example of actual recruiting agencies in the United States. By understanding the importance of effective collaboration, people can stand out from the competition and unleash their career potential.

Why it's important to collaborate effectively with others:
Collaboration is a fundamental aspect of teamwork that allows people to work together towards a common goal. Hiring managers value candidates who can collaborate with others because it demonstrates their ability to communicate, solve problems, and contribute to

team success. In today's connected world, where projects often require cross-functional collaboration, the ability to work well with others is essential.

Benefits of effective collaboration for job seekers:

1. Extended Problem Solving: Collaborating effectively with others allows candidates to draw on diverse perspectives and experiences, leading to more creative and effective problem solving. This skill is highly valued by employers because it demonstrates adaptability and critical thinking.

Case study: Talent Solutions Agency:
The US Talent Solutions Agency specializes in attracting applicants from various industries. They prioritize candidates who can demonstrate the ability to work effectively with others. The agency believes that people who can work well in teams are more likely to succeed in leadership positions and contribute to the overall success of the organization.

2. Improve communication. Collaborating with others requires effective communication skills,

including active listening and clear presentation of ideas. Job seekers who cannot communicate effectively in teams are more likely to face the challenge of building strong relationships and a positive work environment.

Case: Career Connections agency:
The agency is Known for their expertise in the healthcare industry, Career Connections emphasizes the importance of effective collaboration in the hiring process. They note that candidates who are able to communicate and collaborate with others tend to excel in patient care, where teamwork is a key factor in delivering health care services.

3. Increased adaptability: Working effectively with others helps job seekers develop adaptive skills, allowing them to navigate different work environments and take on unexpected challenges. Employers value candidates who can adapt to changing circumstances and actively contribute to team dynamics.

Case study: Professional Edge Agency:
Professional Edge Agency specializes in recruiting

candidates from the technology industry. They found that people who can collaborate effectively with others are more likely to succeed in dynamic and rapidly changing work environments. Their clients often ask for candidates who can adapt to new projects and work in different teams.

Working effectively with others is an essential skill for job seekers looking to unleash their career potential.

Through effective collaboration, people can increase their problem-solving abilities, improve their communication skills, and increase their adaptability.

Recruitment agencies in the United States have recognized the importance of Working effectively with others is an essential skill for job seekers looking to unleash their career potential.

Through effective collaboration, people can increase their problem-solving abilities, improve their communication skills, and increase their adaptability.

Recruitment agencies in the United States have recognized the importance of these skills in the hiring process, re-emphasizing the value of working effectively with others. By mastering this skill, job seekers can stand out from the competition and succeed in their chosen career.

Team Work - Resolving Conflict and Managing Differences

Teamwork skills is essential for professional success. Collaborating effectively with others is not always seamless, as conflicts and misunderstandings are inevitable. However, understanding how to resolve conflicts and deal with disagreements is crucial for job seekers to stand out in their career path. This chapter discusses the importance of conflict resolution and misunderstanding.

The Importance of Resolving Conflicts and Overcoming Differences:

To unlock your career potential and master the communication skills that hiring managers look for, it's important that you understand the value of conflict resolution and dispute management. Effective teamwork is highly valued in the workplace, and your ability to handle conflicts and misunderstandings can set you apart from other job seekers.

Here are some Key Benefits:

Better and more Effective Cooperation: Resolving conflicts and overcoming misunderstandings contribute to creating a harmonious working environment and promoting cooperation among team members. By resolving conflicts quickly and effectively, job seekers can strengthen relationships with colleagues, help with better teamwork, and increase productivity.

Strengthen Professional Relationships: Resolving conflicts and misunderstandings requires effective communication, active listening, and empathy. These skills help job seekers to build strong professional relationships with colleagues, clients, and supervisors. Peaceful conflict resolution increases trust, respect, and understanding among team members.

Strategies for Resolving Conflicts and Overcoming Differences

Job seekers can use a variety of strategies to effectively resolve conflicts and resolve disagreements.

Here are some effective approaches,

Open and Transparent Communication: Encourage clear and honest communication among team members. Create an environment where people feel comfortable expressing their views, concerns, and ideas. This promotes mutual understanding and prevents conflict from escalating.

Active Listening and Empathy: Practice active listening by paying full attention to the other person, try to understand their point of view, and acknowledge their feelings. Empathy plays an important role in conflict resolution because it helps job seekers understand the other person's point of view and find common ground.
Cooperation and Compromise: Encourage

cooperation and seek win-win solutions. By involving all parties in the decision-making process, applicants can find compromises that suit everyone's needs and interests.

Case study: Recruitment Agencies in Brazil
To illustrate the benefits of conflict resolution and dispute management, consider examples from the operation of a Claims Agency in Brazil:

At a recruitment agency in Brazil, a team of recruiters worked on an important project to fill several positions for a client. However, they encountered mixed views on the selection criteria and the listing process. Differences of opinion led to stress and inefficiencies within the group. In recognizing the importance of conflict resolution, the team leader organized a joint discussion so that each team member had a chance to share his or her point of view. Through active listening and empathetic understanding, they identified common goals and came up with a compromise that took into account different perspectives. This collaborative approach not only resolves conflicts, but also strengthens teamwork and improves overall team performance.

Resolving conflicts and overcoming disagreements are important skills that job seekers need to master in order to reach their full career potential.

Real-life examples from recruitment agencies in Brazil show how these skills can help job seekers find work and succeed in the competitive job market.

Teamwork - Support and Encourage Team Members

One of the most important aspects of soft skills is teamwork. Supporting and encouraging team members play an important role in Job Searching. In this chapter, we will discuss the importance of supporting and encouraging team members by providing the tools and strategies to succeed in this area.

Meanwhile, there are various platforms where job seekers can form large groups while looking for work. Some of these forums will be covered in this chapter as we approach our dream job. The support and encouragement of team members benefits not only the overall success of the team, but also the individual candidate. By creating a supportive and encouraging environment, you can create positive team dynamics that increase collaboration, productivity, and job satisfaction. Not only will this improve your team performance, but it will also showcase your leadership and communication skills to potential employers.

So how do you effectively support and encourage team members? Here are some easy ways to consider.

1. Active Listening: Actively listen to the ideas, concerns, and opinions of team members. This shows respect and shows that their opinion is appreciated. By actively listening, you can gain insight, foster open communication, and build a sense of trust within the team.
2. Provide Constructive Feedback.
Give helpful advice to help team members get better and improve. Focus on specific actions,

highlighting both strengths and areas for improvement. Constructive feedback should be given in a supportive and respectful manner, with an emphasis on growth rather than criticism.

3. Recognition of Achievements. Celebrate the good things and accomplishments of your team members. Recognition of their hard work and achievements boosts morale, motivation and overall job satisfaction. This positive reinforcement encourages team members to continue to perform at their best and fosters a culture of appreciation.

4. Provide Support and Resources: Be prepared to provide support and resources to your team members. This could include providing advice, sharing knowledge, or providing access to tools and training. By providing support, you demonstrate your commitment to their success and create an environment where people feel empowered to reach their full potential.

5. Encourage Cooperation. Create a collaborative environment where team members feel comfortable exchanging ideas, collaborating, and

leveraging their strengths. Encouraging collaboration not only fosters creativity and problem-solving, but also fosters solidarity and *camaraderie* within the group.

By using these strategies, you can create a supportive and encouraging dynamic team, which will not only benefit the overall success of the team but also boost your career growth. Job seekers who can support and encourage their team members are in high demand by employers because they demonstrate strong leadership skills, effective communication, and the ability to create an enabling environment.

Remember that supporting and encouraging team members is not only a valuable skill, but a powerful tool for unlocking your career potential. Mastering this aspect of teamwork will set you apart in the job market and make you a highly sought-after candidate for future opportunities.

Job seekers can connect and support each other in many different ways and on different platforms. Here are a few suggestions,

1. Online Jobs Search Community: Join online communities and job search forums. Sites like LinkedIn, Reddit, or specialized job search platforms often have special groups where job seekers can connect, share experiences, and support each other. Participate in discussions, ask questions and help other job seekers.

2. Networking Events: Attend networking events, job fairs or industry conferences where you can meet other job seekers. Connect, share information and support each other. These events give you the opportunity to expand your professional network and reach potential clients through recommendations.

3. Job Search Club. Join a job search club or create one in your area. These clubs bring together people who are actively looking for work. Members can share potential job openings, exchange tips, conduct test interviews, and provide emotional support during the job search.

4. Alumni Network. Take advantage of your institution's alumni network. Many universities

and colleges have alumni associations or online platforms where alumni can network. Reach out to graduates who are also looking for work and provide support, share recommendations or potential job offers.

5. Online Collaboration Tools. Use online collaboration tools like Google Drive, Trello, or Slack to create virtual job search teams. These platforms allow job seekers to share resources, collaborate on job applications, provide feedback on resumes and cover letters, and provide support throughout the job search.

6. Professional Associations: Join professional associations or organizations related to your area of interest. These associations often have membership directories, online forums, or networking events where you can connect with other professionals in your field. Connect with other members, attend events and participate in mentoring programs for guidance and support.

Remember that when working with other candidates, it is important to approach the relationship in a spirit of mutual support and cooperation. Be ready to share your knowledge, experience and resources, and be ready to receive help and advice in return.

Building a support network of other job seekers can provide potential motivation, understanding and guidance, making the job search process more manageable and less isolated.

Here are the ways and platforms that job seekers can come together to support each other:

1. LinkedIn Groups.
2. Reddit community (e.g. r/jobs, r/careeradvice).
3. Job Search Forums (eg: Indeed, Glassdoor).
4. Facebook-job search group.
5. Twitter chats and hashtags (ex: #JobSearchChat, #CareerAdvice).
6. Meetup.com, job search event.
7. Local job seekers support groups or clubs.
8. Connection events and alumni platform.

9. Professional networking, events and conferences.
10. Online job search community (e.g. Jobcase, CareerOneStop).
11. Industry Forums and Discussion Forums.
12. Virtual job fairs and job fairs.
13. Online mentoring programs for job-seekers.
14. Online job search software.
15. Webinars and Job Search Workshops.
16. Volunteer or do internships in professional organizations.
17. Online coaching or career counseling groups.
18. Local community centers that provide job search assistance.
19. Online mastermind groups for candidates.
20. Dedicated apps or job search platform with social features.

These platforms and opportunities offer job seekers the chance to network, share resources, share advice, and support each other throughout their job search. Make sure to actively participate in discussions, and build valuable connections to maximize the benefits of these collaborative environments.

Time Management

In the dynamic and difficult competitive environment of the modern labor market, time management is of great importance. When you're on your way to unleashing your career potential, mastering the art of time management becomes paramount. This chapter discusses the importance of effective time management and provides practical strategies for improving this important skill.

Time management is a powerful principle that allows people to manage their time wisely, allowing them to maximize their productivity and achieve their goals. It involves a variety of techniques, including prioritizing, careful planning, and effective task organization. By improving your time management skills, you can achieve more in your limited time, practically reduce your stress levels, and dramatically increase your chances of landing your dream job.

One of the main advantages of time management

for job seekers is its ability to facilitate organization. The job search process often involves multiple tasks, such as finding companies, networking, writing resumes, and attending interviews. ***Without effective time management, it is easy to miss important deadlines and opportunities.***

By implementing proven time management strategies, you can create a structured plan, set clear goals, and ensure you stay on top of your job search activities.

Another advantage of time management is the ability to focus attention. In an age characterized by constant digital distractions, staying focused on important tasks can be a challenge. However, with good time management, you can minimize distractions, prioritize activities, and spend uninterrupted time on important activities like finding a job, preparing for an interview, or improving on your skills. This not only increases your productivity but also demonstrates your commitment and dedication to potential employers.

Additionally, effective time management plays an important role in maintaining a healthy work-life balance. Finding a job often requires a significant amount of time, including extensive research, attending networking events, and plenty of interviews. Without proper time management, it is easy to neglect personal relationships, hobbies, and self-care.

When you make out time for both your job search and personal pursuits, you can find a harmonious balance, minimize burnout, and present yourself to employers as a versatile candidate.

In this chapter, we'll cover a variety of time management techniques, including planning, setting goals, prioritizing tasks, and harnessing the power of technology.

Using these strategies will not only improve your job search performance, but also develop a valuable skill set that will serve you throughout your career.

Time is an invaluable resource and mastering the art of time management is to unlock your career potential. So let's embark on this journey together, learning how to optimize your time, use every opportunity to excel in the job search and ultimately unleash your true potential.

Prioritizing Tasks and Completing Work on Time

In today's competitive and strong labor market, the mastery of the art of arranging priorities and performances is necessary for professional success. In this section, " Unlocking Career Opportunities: The Power of Soft Skills in Job Searching," investigating the importance of work, Manage effective time and provide practical strategies to help people succeed in their career.

1. The importance of prioritizing work: Prioritizing tasks involves determining the order in which to do them based on their importance and urgency. By understanding the importance of each task, everyone can allocate time and resources more efficiently; ensuring important tasks are completed on time.

2. Task priority strategy
a) Assess Task Importance: This strategy involves evaluating tasks based on their impact on long-term goals, project timelines, and overall goals organizations. By assigning high-priority tasks,

everyone can allocate their time and efforts appropriately; ensuring important tasks are completed on time.

b) Analyze the urgency of the task. Urgency refers to the time sensitivity of the task. This strategy includes identifying tasks with unavoidable deadlines or those that need immediate attention. By recognizing urgent tasks, people can prioritize their workload and avoid unnecessary delays.

c) Apply the 80/20 rule. The Pareto Principle, also called the 80/20 rule, says that most of the outcomes come from a small portion of the work. By focusing on the most important tasks that contribute to meaningful results, people can optimize their productivity and time management.

3. Method of working on time:

A) The installation of practical terms: Setting practical terms is important for effective time management.

b) Break down tasks: Large projects or tasks can be overwhelming. *Breaking them down into smaller, manageable tasks not only makes them less complicated,* but also allows everyone to track progress and meet deadlines more efficiently.

c) Avoid procrastination. Procrastination can reduce productivity and lead to late deadlines.

4. Benefits for job seekers.
The ability to prioritize and complete work on time is highly appreciated by employers. Job seekers who demonstrate good time management skills see themselves as reliable, efficient, and competent professionals. Prioritizing tasks and getting things done on time are important parts of effective time management.

By applying the strategies and methods described in this section, people can reach their full career potential. Whether you're a recent graduate entering the job market or a seasoned professional looking to advance your career, mastering time management skills will set you apart. Differentiate and pave the way to success in today's competitive environment.

Find here some benefits of prioritizing tasks and getting things done on time as a job seeker:

1. Improve your professional reputation: Demonstrating good time management skills during your job search can help build a positive professional reputation. Employers value candidates who are reliable, punctual, and able to meet deadlines. While displaying the ability to identify priorities in tasks and perform the work on time, you're set up as a reliable and organized expert.

2. Increase efficiency and productivity. Effective time management allows job seekers to optimize their productivity. By prioritizing tasks, you can focus on the activities that matter most and are most productive, ensuring you get the most out of your time and effort. This increased efficiency not only helps you fill out job applications and prepare for interviews quickly, but it also allows you to multi-task without feeling overwhelmed.

3. Reduce stress and improve work-life balance. Finding a job can be a stressful process, but effective time management can help alleviate some of that stress. By prioritizing tasks and managing your time effectively, you can avoid the last-minute rush and accompanying anxiety. This allows for a healthier work-life balance, allowing time for self-care, recreation and other hobbies, as well as finding a job.

4. Show self-discipline and organizational skills. Employers value candidates with self-discipline and strong organizational skills. By effectively prioritizing tasks and completing tasks on time, you demonstrate your ability to plan, organize, and fulfill responsibilities. This demonstrates your professionalism and ability to work independently, making you an attractive candidate for potential employers.

5. Increase the effectiveness of job interviews. Prioritizing and completing tasks on time also positively affects the effectiveness of the conversation. By managing your time effectively,

you'll be able to thoroughly prepare for interviews, research campaigns, and practice answering behavior-based interview questions. This level of preparation boosts your confidence, allows you to showcase your skills and experience more effectively, and increases your chances of impressing employers.

6. Competitive advantage in the labor market. With good time management skills, you will gain a competitive edge over other job seekers. Employers are looking for candidates who can multitask, meet deadlines, and deliver results. By emphasizing your ability to prioritize and get work done on time, you position yourself as a valuable asset to potential employers, setting you apart from other candidates.

I included these benefits here to help job seekers understand the value of prioritizing tasks and getting things done on time when looking for a job. It highlights the importance of effective time management as an important communication skill that can greatly increase their chances of getting a job offer and helping them advance in their career.

Some views on how job seekers can prioritize and get tasks done on time while looking for work.

1. Plan your job search: Start by creating a comprehensive job search plan that includes all required tasks and deadlines. Break the process down into smaller, more manageable steps, such as updating your resume, searching for a company, networking, and applying for offers. Sort these tasks by their level of importance and urgency.

2. Identify high-priority opportunities: Focus on job opportunities that are closely related to your skills, qualifications, and career goals. Thoroughly research companies and jobs to determine which best fit for you. By prioritizing quality over quantity, you can invest your time and effort in apps that have a higher chance of success.

3. Set realistic goals and deadlines. Set realistic goals and deadlines for each task in your job search plan. Be aware of your abilities and the

time it takes to complete each task efficiently. Setting achievable deadlines helps you stay organized, motivated and complete tasks on time, avoiding unnecessary stress and last-minute rush.
4. Use time management techniques. Use time management techniques to optimize your productivity. Techniques such as the Pomodoro Technique (focused work with short breaks) or time blocking (setting specific intervals for different tasks) can help you stay in place, manage your time efficiently and complete tasks on time.

5. Prioritize building networks and relationships. Organize these tasks according to their importance and urgency. Take the time to network with experts in your industry; attend networking events and rewarding interviews. By prioritizing relationships, you can tap into potential job openings, gain valuable insights, and increase your chances of landing the right job.

6. Stay Organized with Task Management Tools: Utilize task management tools or apps to keep track of your job search tasks, deadlines, and

progress. These tools can help you prioritize tasks, set reminders, and ensure that nothing falls through the cracks. By staying organized, you can efficiently manage your workload and complete tasks on time.

7. Avoid Procrastination: Procrastination can hinder your job search progress. Recognize and address any tendencies to procrastinate by breaking tasks into smaller, more manageable steps. Set specific deadlines for each task and hold yourself accountable. Utilize techniques like visualization, creating to-do lists, or seeking an accountability partner to stay motivated and focused.

8. Seek Support and Feedback: Don't hesitate to seek support from mentors, career counselors, or trusted friends and family members. They can provide guidance, offer feedback on your resume and cover letter, and help you stay motivated throughout your job search. Their perspectives and insights can help you prioritize tasks effectively and make informed decisions.

It is good that job hunters implement these views and strategies, prioritize their tasks, manage their time effectively, and complete their job search activities promptly. This approach will increase their chances of finding suitable job opportunities, securing interviews, and ultimately landing their desired job.

Manage Your Schedule and Stay Focused

This chapter explores the subtopic of managing your schedule and focus, and provides practical strategies and tips to help you be more productive and successful. By mastering these skills, job seekers can demonstrate their ability to prioritize tasks, achieve set goals, and excel in their career endeavors.

In the world of job hunting, efficient schedule management and relentless focus are essential to achieving optimal results. Here we look at valuable techniques to help you organize your schedule and stay focused amid distractions as a job seeker.

1. Strategy to Prioritize Tasks: To effectively manage your schedule, it's important to prioritize tasks based on their urgency and importance. Using a framework like the Eisenhower Matrix, candidates can divide tasks into four parts: urgent and important, important but not urgent, urgent but not important, and neither urgent nor important. This approach allows people to allocate time and energy efficiently, focusing on the tasks that bring the most value.

The Eisenhower Matrix, also known as the Eisenhower Decision Matrix, is a productivity tool that helps people prioritize tasks and make effective decisions. It is named after President Dwight D. Eisenhower, who is known for his ability to effectively manage time and responsibilities.

The grid is divided into four quadrants according to two criteria: urgency and importance. Urgency refers to the time sensitivity of a task, while importance refers to its impact on long-term goals and overall success.

The four quadrants of the Eisenhower matrix:

(a) Important and Urgent: Issues in this quadrant require immediate attention and must be addressed immediately. As a rule, these are important tasks that cannot be postponed.

(b) Important but not urgent: Tasks in this quadrant are important to long-term success but do not have an immediate deadline. They require proactive planning and must be prioritized so they don't become urgent later.

(c) Urgent but ineffective. Tasks in this quadrant are often urgent, but do not contribute significantly to long-term goals. They are often distractions or obstacles that can be delegated or removed to free up time for more important tasks.

(d) Not important and not urgent: Tasks in this quadrant are low priority and should be kept to a minimum or eliminated whenever possible. They are often a waste of time or trivial tasks that don't contribute to your goals or productivity.

Using the Eisenhower Matrix, people can effectively prioritize their tasks and focus on what really matters. This helps avoid procrastination, reduces stress, and achieves a better work-life balance.

2. Set Clear and Achievable Goals: Making clear and achievable goals is an important part of managing time effectively. Job seekers should set SMART goals – specific, measurable, achievable, relevant and on time – to provide direction and motivation. By breaking down larger goals into smaller, achievable steps, people can better manage their schedules and track their progress.

Creating specific and doable objectives is a basic part of managing time well. A popular goal setting plan is the SMART method. SMART indicates "Specific, Measurable, Achievable, Relevant and Timely".

Let's look at each element and see how it can help job seekers manage their schedule and stay focused.

1. Specifically: Specificity is important when setting goals. Instead of a vague goal like "improve communication skills", the specific goal would be "take a public speaking course to improve presentation skills". By clearly defining what you want to achieve, you set yourself a specific goal that you are striving for. Specific goals help guide your actions and allow you to allocate time and resources efficiently.

2. Measurable: Measurable goals are essential to track progress and stay motivated. When setting goals, set specific criteria that allow you to measure your success. For example, if your goal is to grow your customer base, you might set a measurable goal of acquiring five new customers in a given time frame. Measuring your progress keeps you focused and gives you a sense of accomplishment as you hit milestones on your journey.

Another block of time could be dedicated to networking activities. This could involve reaching out to contacts, attending virtual or in-person networking events, or engaging with industry professionals on social media platforms.

You can also allocate time to updating your resume, tailoring it to specific job applications, and writing compelling cover letters. By dedicating specific time slots for these tasks, you ensure that you're actively working towards your job-seeking goals and not getting overwhelmed or distracted by other activities.

Time blocking helps you prioritize your job-seeking activities and ensures that you're making progress each day. It helps in managing your time effectively, staying focused, and ultimately increasing your chances of finding a job that aligns with your goals and aspirations.

Mastering time management is a critical skill for job seekers, and managing your schedule and staying focused are integral components of this discipline. By strategically prioritizing tasks, setting clear goals, utilizing technology tools, creating a structured routine, minimizing distractions, and practicing effective time blocking, job seekers can optimize their schedules and excel in their professional pursuits. Remember, effective time management not only enhances productivity but also demonstrates your ability to handle responsibilities and meet deadlines, making you a valuable asset to any employer.

3. Can be achieved: It's important to set goals that are challenging but also possible to reach. Consider your current resources, skills, and limitations when setting goals. When we set goals that are not realistic, it can make us feel frustrated and less motivated. Assess your skills and set goals that will challenge you but won't overwhelm you. By setting achievable goals for yourself, you increase your chances of success and maintain a positive attitude along the way.

4. Fact: Relevance is the alignment of your goals with your overall career goals. Ensure that the goals you set align with the desired outcome and

contribute to your career growth. Think about how each goal fits into the big picture and how it can help you advance in your career. By setting the right goals, you focus on what really matters and don't waste time on tasks that don't align with your long-term aspirations.

5. Time is limited: Planning is crucial for effective schedule management. Timed goals create a sense of urgency and help prioritize tasks. Set a specific time frame for each goal, be it weekly, monthly or yearly. By breaking down big goals into smaller, time-bound milestones, you can track your progress and make adjustments along the way. Deadlines also act as a powerful motivator, forcing you to stay focused and act consistently.

By incorporating the SMART goal framework into your goal-setting process, you gain clarity, motivation, and direction. This approach ensures that your goals are specific, measurable, achievable, and timed for success. In managing your schedule and focus, be sure to regularly review and adjust your goals as needed to accommodate changing circumstances or new opportunities that may present themselves.

SMART Setting Goals is a powerful tool for job seekers to manage their schedule and stay focused.

By setting specific, measurable, achievable, relevant, and time-bound goals, people can effectively allocate time and resources, track their progress, and stay on track motivated. Incorporate the SMART Goal Framework into your goal setting and watch your productivity and success grow. Remember, it's not just about setting goals; it's about setting goals that align with your aspirations and help you move forward in your career.

3. Using technology tools: In the digital age, technology provides many tools to help you manage your schedule. Using a calendar application, task management software, or project management platform can provide a visual representation of your schedule, allowing you to allocate time to specific tasks and follow your schedule or deadline tracks. In addition, these tools often provide reminders and notifications to help you stay on top of things.

4. Create a structured routine: Establishing an organized routine is crucial to maintaining focus and maximizing productivity. ***Identify your most productive hours*** and break them down into tasks that require intense attention and focus. Plus, taking regular breaks in your schedule can help prevent burnout and keep you productive throughout the day.

5. Minimize distractions: In the age of constant communication, distractions can easily disrupt your schedule and focus. Minimize disturbance by blocking notifications on your device, determining the specified time to read emails or being on social media, as well as creating a special workspace that contribute to high level of focus. Set a clear boundary to protect valuable time.

6. Practice effective time management: Time blocking is an effective technique for allocating specific time intervals to different activities. By scheduling blocks of time allotted for specific tasks, meetings, and personal commitments, job seekers can accurately understand their schedules, prioritize effectively, and avoid over

commitment. This way, we make sure to give each task the attention it needs.

Time blocking is a time management technique in which you set aside specific periods of time for different activities or tasks. This includes planning your day or week in advance and allocating specific time periods for specific activities. In the context of a job search, time blocking can be extremely helpful. When looking for a job, you have to perform various tasks such as finding companies, making contacts, updating resumes, and applying for jobs. Time blocking allows you to allocate time to each of these tasks, ensuring you give them the attention they deserve.

For example, you can allocate a certain amount of time each day to research and identify potential vacancies. During this time, you can browse job boards, company websites and professional networking platforms to find the right job.

Another block of time could be dedicated to networking activities. This could involve reaching out to contacts, attending virtual or in-person networking events, or engaging with industry professionals on social media platforms.

You can also allocate time for updating your resume, tailoring it to specific job applications, and writing compelling cover letters. By dedicating specific time slots for these tasks, you ensure that you're actively working towards your job-seeking goals and not getting overwhelmed or distracted by other activities.

Time blocking helps you prioritize your job-seeking activities and ensures that you're making progress each day. It helps in managing your time effectively, staying focused, and ultimately increasing your chances of finding a job that aligns with your goals and aspirations. Mastering time management is a critical skill for job seekers, and managing your schedule and staying focused are integral components of this discipline. By strategically prioritizing tasks, setting clear goals, utilizing technology tools, creating a structured routine, minimizing distractions, and practicing effective time blocking, job seekers can optimize their schedules and excel in their professional pursuits. Remember, effective time management not only enhances productivity but also demonstrates your ability to handle responsibilities and meet deadlines, making you a valuable asset to any employer.

Mastering Efficiency and Productivity: A Guide for Job Seekers

To stand out from the crowd and secure their dream job, individuals must effectively manage their time, tasks, and resources. This chapter aims to provide valuable insights and actionable strategies to help job seekers enhance their performance and productivity throughout the job search process.

The Power of Time Management: Efficiently allocating time for different activities can significantly impact productivity. Time blocking, a popular technique, involves scheduling specific time slots for various tasks such as researching job opportunities, networking, and updating resumes. By dedicating focused time to each task, job seekers can avoid distractions and ensure progress toward their goals. Prioritizing tasks using the Eisenhower Matrix helps identify urgent activities, enabling job seekers to make informed decisions and tackle critical tasks first. Effective time management enhances productivity, reduces stress, and maximizes the chances of securing a job.

Streamlining Job Search Efforts:

To be efficient and productive in the job search, job seekers must streamline their efforts. This involves leveraging technology and tools to their advantage. Online job boards and professional networking platforms provide a vast array of opportunities and connections.

By utilizing research filters and setting up job alerts, job seekers can narrow down their search and focus on relevant positions. Maintaining a well-organized digital presence, such as an updated LinkedIn profile, helps attract potential employers. Using productivity tools like project control software or task management apps can help job seekers stay coordinated, track progress, and meet deadlines.

Developing Effective Performance Habits: Personal work habits also influenced efficiency and productivity. Job seekers should cultivate habits that optimize their performance. This includes setting realistic goals, breaking them down into manageable tasks, and setting periods. Reviewing progress and adjusting strategies ensures continuous improvement.

Practicing effective communication skills, both written and verbal, is crucial for conveying professionalism and making a positive impression on potential employers. Adopting a growth mindset, embracing challenges, and seeking feedback are likewise essential for personal and professional development.

Being efficient is key for job seekers in navigating the competitive job market. By mastering time management, streamlining work search efforts, and developing effective work habits, individuals can enhance their productivity and increase their chances of securing their dream careers.

Adaptability: Accepting Change and Succeeding in the Labor Market

In the context of a dynamic labor market, adaptability has become an essential skill for job seekers. With the growth of industries, technological advancements changing the working process, and economic uncertainty, adaptability has become essential for career success. This article explores the concept of adaptability and provides valuable insights and strategies to help job seekers navigate successfully in the ever-changing employment landscape.

Understand the power of adaptability: As the labor market continues to evolve, adaptability has become a trait that employers value highly. The ability to embrace change, learn new skills, and navigate unfamiliar situations is critical to staying competitive. Recognizing the importance of adaptability, job seekers can position themselves as a valuable asset by demonstrating the ability to thrive in a variety of work environments.

Developing adaptive thinking: The development of adaptive thinking is the basis of adaptability and effectiveness. This includes developing a growth-oriented attitude, accepting challenges, and maintaining a positive attitude. Job hunters with an adaptive mindset will be better prepared to overcome obstacles, overcome setbacks, and seize opportunities. By developing this mindset, people can show potential employers that they are resilient and flexible.

Customize your skill set for success: In an ever-changing job market, job applicants must tailor their skills to meet the needs of employers. Identifying transferable skills and using them effectively is basic to demonstrating flexibility. In addition, continuous learning and development play a key role in adapting to changes in the industry. By proactively updating and expanding their skill sets, job seekers can increase their chances of being hired and demonstrate a commitment to career growth.

Accept change and deal with uncertainty: Change and uncertainty are inherent aspects of any career path. Career seekers who accept change and see uncertainty as an opportunity for growth are more likely to succeed. People who adapt quickly to new circumstances, are flexible in their approach, and are resilient in the face of challenges. By embracing change and facing uncertainty confidently, prospective employees can demonstrate their ability to thrive in a dynamic work environment.

Show adaptability in interviews and resumes: Job searchers should emphasize their adaptability in interviews and CVs. Sharing compelling stories that show how they have successfully adapted to difficult situations can make a lasting impression on potential employers. Furthermore, including responsiveness-related keywords and phrases in your CV can improve visibility and increase your chances of getting a Candidate Tracking System (ATS) attention.

In a rapidly changing labor market, adaptability and productivity are significant to prosperity and success. Job prospects can position themselves as highly desirable candidates. Adjustment efficiency gives people the confidence to navigate the ever-changing world of work and land their dream job.

Adaptation to change and flexibility: key skills of job seekers

Welcome to this comprehensive guide to adapting to change and flexibility, designed specifically for job seekers. In today's rapidly changing job market, adaptability and flexibility have become a key success factor. This article examines the importance of these skills, offers practical strategies for developing them, and provides valuable tips to help job seekers navigate successfully in the ever-changing job market.

Understand the importance of adapting to change: In a world driven by technological progress and evolving industries, change is inevitable. Job seekers who can adapt to new circumstances and accept change are more likely to succeed. Job providers' value people who can quickly learn new skills, adapt to changing priorities, and thrive in a dynamic work environment. Recognizing the importance of adapting to change is the first step to building a successful career.

The power of flexibility in the labor market: Flexibility is a much sought-after skill in today's job market. Employers appreciate candidates who can adapt their schedules, tasks, and approach to changing needs. Flexibility allows candidates to deal with unexpected challenges, take on new responsibilities, and effectively contribute to team dynamics. This demonstrates a willingness to go one step further and a commitment to achieving the organization's goals.

Develop adaptability and flexibility

1. Adopt a growth mindset. Developing a growth

mindset is essential to developing adaptability and resilience. See adversity as an opportunity to grow, see failure as a learning experience, and stay optimistic about change.

2. Expand your skill set: Constantly learning new skills and keeping up with industry trends increases your adaptability. Look for degree programs, online courses, and career opportunities to expand your skill set and adapt to changing job demands.

3. Highlight transferable skills: Identify and highlight your transferable skills – skills that can be applied to a variety of roles and industries. These skills, such as communication, problem-solving, and leadership, demonstrate your flexibility and adaptability to potential employers.

4. Use new technology. Stay up to date with the latest technologies in your field and be ready to use them in your work. Demonstrate proficiency in the right software, tools, and digital platforms that demonstrate your ability to adapt to employer requirements.

5. Connect and seek opinions. Join professional networks and seek feedback from mentors, peers, and industry experts. This will help you gain

different perspectives, learn from the experiences of others, and tailor your approach based on valuable insights.

Navigate change and uncertainty
1. Stay informed: Stay up to date with industry trends, economic changes, and technological advancements. This knowledge will help you anticipate changes and proactively adapt to them.
2. Anticipate and plan: Make contingency plans and prepare for unexpected changes. This proactive approach allows you to react quickly and effectively to new situations.

3. Flexibility: Be open to new ideas, different ways of working, and alternative solutions. Embrace flexibility in your thinking and be ready to explore non-traditional approaches to problem-solving.
4. Develop resilience: Resilience is essential to adapt to change. Develop coping mechanisms, practice self-care, and cultivate a positive attitude to recover from setbacks and confidently navigate uncertainty.

Problem Solving and Decision Making: Key Job Search Skills

Employers are looking for candidates with not only technical knowledge but also good decision-making and problem-solving skills. These skills are vital to overcoming adversity, making informed decisions, and achieving success in the workplace. In this article, we explore the importance of problem-solving and decision-making skills for job seekers, and provide practical tips on how to improve these skills.

Understand how to troubleshoot: Problem solving is the process of identifying, analyzing, and solving problems or obstacles that arise in different work situations. Employers appreciate people who can approach problems with a positive mindset and find effective solutions. Job seekers should take a structured approach to learning how to solve problems.

1. Define complexity: Be clear about the problem, making sure you fully understand its impact and

scope.

2. Gather information: Collect all relevant data and facts related to the problem to get a full picture of the situation.

3. Generate alternatives: brainstorm potential solutions or approaches to problem solving, encourage creativity, and consider different points of view.

4. Evaluate options: Evaluate the pros and cons of each potential solution, weighing their feasibility, cost-effectiveness, and potential outcomes.

5. Implement Selected Solution: Take action on the selected Solution, ensure efficient implementation and track progress.

6. Reflect and learn: After implementing a solution, evaluate its effectiveness and draw lessons for future troubleshooting efforts.

Develop decision-making skills: Decision making is closely related to problem solving as it involves choosing the best course of action from available alternatives. Employers are looking for candidates who can make informed and effective decisions.

Here are some strategies to improve your decision-making skills.

1. Situational analysis: Gather all the necessary information and evaluate the possible consequences of each decision. Consider short- and long-term impacts on stakeholders and the organization as a whole.
2. Use critical thinking: Apply logical thinking and critical thinking skills to assess the strengths and weaknesses of each alternative. Consider both quantitative and qualitative factors to make informed decisions.
3. Seek opinion: Consult a colleague, mentor, or subject matter expert to get different perspectives and ideas. This collaborative approach can help identify blind spots and provide innovative solutions.
4. Set priorities and set goals. Clearly define the desired outcomes and rank them according to their importance and urgency. This will help guide the decision-making process and ensure alignment with the organization's goals.

5. Take calculated risks. Decision making often

requires weighing potential risks and benefits. Be prepared to step out of your comfort zone and take calculated risks if necessary, taking into account possible mitigations.

6. Think about past decisions. Evaluate the results of your decisions regularly and think about what went well and what could have been done differently. Such self-reflection contributes to continuous improvement and personal growth.

7. Influencing Candidates. Job seekers with good decision-making and problem-solving skills will have a competitive edge in the job market. Employers recognize that these skills contribute to a candidate's ability to handle difficult situations, adapt to change, and contribute to the overall success of the organization. By highlighting these skills in resumes, interviews, and cover letters, job seekers can prove their worth and stand out from other candidates. Problem-solving and decision-making skills are essential for job seekers who want to excel in their careers. Thanks to a structured approach to problem solving and streamlining decision-making, individuals can demonstrate an ability to cope with challenges and contribute to their employer's success.

Continuous practice, reflection and feedback seeking will further improve these skills, allowing job seekers to stand out in the competitive job market.

Emphasizing these skills during the job search will help the candidate land in the desired position and achieve career success.

Learning and Growing through Experience: A Guide for Job Seekers

It is important that candidates not only possess the required qualifications, but also demonstrate a growth-oriented attitude and willingness to learn from experience. This article is intended to provide valuable information and practical advice to job seekers on how to use their experience to improve their employability and achieve career growth.

1. Apply growth mindset: One of the key qualities that employers look for in candidates is a growth mindset. This mindset includes the belief that abilities and intelligence can be developed through dedication and hard work. A growth mindset allows job seekers to see challenges as opportunities to grow and learn. By adopting this mindset, people can approach their job search with resilience and a determination to continuously improve.

2. Consider experience: Before you start looking for a job, take some time to reflect on your experience. Take into account skills, knowledge, and achievements gained in previous positions, internships or volunteering. Reflecting on these experiences will help identify transferable skills that can be emphasized in interviews and resumes. It is also an opportunity to identify areas for improvement and personal growth.

3. Use universal skills: Transferable skills are things you're good at that you can use in lots of different jobs and fields. These skills include communication, problem solving, teamwork, leadership, and adaptability.

Candidates should identify and highlight their transferable skills when writing resumes and in interviews. By demonstrating these skills, candidates can demonstrate their ability to quickly adapt to new environments and add value to potential employers.

4. Look for continuous learning opportunities: In a rapidly changing job market, job seekers must demonstrate a commitment to constant learning. Stay up to date with emerging industry trends, advancements, and technologies with continued education courses, seminars, webinars, and industry conferences. Not only will this improve your knowledge and skills, but it will also show potential employers your commitment to staying relevant in your field.

5. Focus on growth and learning in interviews: During the interview, it's important to emphasize your growth mindset and willingness to learn. Share examples of how you have faced challenges, learned from them, and applied these lessons to positive results. Employers value candidates who can demonstrate a proactive approach to personal and professional development.

6. Accept feedback: Getting feedback is an invaluable opportunity for growth. Whether it's feedback from a mentor, colleague, or hiring

manager, it provides insights into areas for improvement and helps improve skills and performance. Accept constructive criticism and use it as a catalyst for personal growth. Demonstrating your ability to accept and implement feedback shows the employer that you are open to continuous growth and improvement.

Learning and growing through experience is essential for job seekers. By adopting a growth mindset, reflecting on experience, using transferable skills, seeking continuous learning opportunities, emphasizing growth in interviews, and leveraging feedback, you can increase employability and career development. Don't forget that every experience, good or bad, is a chance to learn and get better. Take advantage of these opportunities and you will be successful on your job search and beyond.

Unleash Your Leadership Potential: a Guide for Job Seekers

Strong leadership skills is a key differentiator for candidates. Employers are constantly looking for people who not only perform their roles perfectly but also inspire and motivate others. This article aims to provide job seekers with practical ideas and strategies for developing and manifesting their leadership potential, which will ultimately increase their chances of landing their dream job.

1. Understanding leadership: Before diving into the practical aspects, it is important to understand the nature of leadership. Being a leader doesn't just mean having a fancy job title or being in charge. It means having the right attitude and knowing how to do things well.

Having good emotional intelligence is really important for being a leader.
Being a leader means having the right attitude and knowing how to do things well. Effective leaders possess qualities such as excellent communication, problem-solving, adaptability, and a strong sense of integrity.

2. Self-esteem: To be a successful leader, it's important to start with understanding yourself. Conducting a thorough self-assessment allows candidates to identify strengths and areas for improvement. Reflecting on past experiences, both personal and professional, can provide valuable insights into your leadership potential.

3. Leadership development
A. Communication skills: Effective communication is the foundation of leadership. Job seekers should focus on improving oral and written communication skills as well as active listening skills. Clear and concise communication ensures understanding and effective implementation of ideas.

B. Emotional Intelligence: Having good emotional intelligence is really important for being a leader. Understanding and managing your emotions, as well as empathy for others, will improve interpersonal relationships and contribute to a positive work environment. Job seekers should strive to develop their emotional intelligence through self-awareness and empathy exercises.

C. Problem-solving and decision-making: Leaders often face complex challenges that require critical thinking and decision-making skills. Job seekers need to demonstrate the ability to analyze problems, come up with creative solutions, and make informed decisions. Highlighting past experiences where they were able to solve problems can significantly improve their leadership profile.

4. Demonstrating Leadership Potential

a. CV and cover letter. Candidates should customize their resume and cover letter to highlight their leadership experience and achievements. Include specific examples of leadership roles, projects, or initiatives taken that demonstrate their ability to take responsibility and make a positive impact.

b. Prepare for the interview. Before the interview, candidates should familiarize themselves with the company's culture and values to tailor their response to the organization's expectations. They should be prepared to discuss situations in which they demonstrate leadership qualities, such as leading a team, resolving conflict, or promoting positive change.

Draw Network: Building a strong professional network is a valuable asset for job seekers. Participating in industry events, joining relevant professional associations, and participating in online networking platforms can provide the opportunity to demonstrate leadership potential and connect with potential employers.

In the modern job market, employers have a great need for leadership qualities. Candidates who can effectively demonstrate their leadership potential will have a competitive advantage over other candidates. By understanding leadership, self-assessment, core leadership skills, and demonstrating their potential through resumes, interviews, and networking, job seekers can dramatically increase visibility and win the chances of landing a dream job.

a. Remember that leadership is not limited to one title; it is a way of thinking and a set of skills that can be developed and used in different professional situations. Unleash your leadership potential and unlock unlimited career opportunities.

Inspire and Motivate Others: Unleash your Potential for Career Success

Having the right skills and qualifications is important for job seekers, but it's equally important for them to stand out from the crowd. One way to do this is to inspire and motivate others, which can lead to empowerment and career success. Under this topic, we look at effective strategies and techniques for inspiring and motivating others, making you a sought-after candidate.

1. The Power of a Positive Attitude: When it comes to inspiring and motivating others, it's important to keep a positive attitude. Employers are attracted to candidates with a positive and optimistic attitude. By focusing on the positive aspects of your experience and highlighting your strengths, you will not only inspire those around you, but also make a lasting impression on potential employers.

2. Communicate Effectively: Communication is the key to successful interaction and collaboration. By developing excellent communication skills, you can inspire and motivate others to achieve their best. Active listening, clear pronunciation, and empathy are important components of effective communication. By actively interacting with others and understanding their needs, you can inspire them to achieve their goals while creating a positive work environment.

3. Lead by Examples: Leading by example is a good way to inspire and motivate others. By demonstrating integrity, dedication, and professionalism in your actions, you can inspire others to follow suit. This is true not only at work, but also in our everyday lives. Being a role model in every aspect of your life will help you inspire others and have a positive impact on their lives.

4. Encourage Cooperation: Collaboration is essential to success in any business. By creating an atmosphere of collaboration, you can inspire and motivate others to work together towards a common goal. Encourage open communication, respect different points of view, and encourage teamwork. In this way, you not only inspire others, but you also create a supportive and productive work culture.

5. Recognition and Celebration of Achievements: Recognition and celebration of achievement is a powerful motivator. Recognition of the efforts and achievements of colleagues, team members, and even competitors can inspire them to strive

for excellence. Celebrate important events, appreciate when necessary, and build a culture of gratitude. In this way, you will inspire others to expand their possibilities and reach their full potential.

6. Lifelong Learning and Personal Development: Inspiring and motivating others require continuous learning and personal development. Stay up to date with industry trends, learn new skills, and share your knowledge with others. By demonstrating a growth mindset and thirst for knowledge, you will inspire others to do the same. Take advantage of career development opportunities and encourage others to do the same.

In the current landscape of a highly competitive job market, the ability to inspire and motivate others is of paramount importance and a valuable skill that can set you apart from other job seekers. By developing a positive attitude, communicating effectively, setting a leading example, encouraging collaboration, recognizing achievement, and engaging in continuous learning, you can inspire and motivate others to succeed. Remember, by inspiring others, you are not only benefiting them, but also positively affecting your life and career. So go ahead and inspire others to reach their full potential and success will surely follow.

Communicating Vision and Goals: A Roadmap to Career Success

In an ever-changing job market, effective communication is an essential skill for job seekers. In this part of the book, we'll look at the importance of communicating your vision and goals and how it can propel your career forward. When you understand the power of clear and persuasive communication, you'll be able to effectively communicate your aspirations and ambitions to potential employers, setting you apart from the competition.

1. Create a Compelling Vision: A compelling vision serves as a guiding light not only for you but also

for those with whom you interact. Start by defining your long-term goals and aspirations, and then build them into a clear and concise vision. This will help you communicate your passion and purpose to the employer by demonstrating your commitment and dedication.

2. Alignment of Goals with Organizational Goals: To effectively communicate your goals, it's important that they align with the goals of the organization you're targeting. Review the company's mission, values, and strategic initiatives to ensure your goals align with their vision. This alignment shows that you understand the company's direction and that you can contribute to its success.

3. Develop a Persuasive Communication Style: How you communicate your vision and goals can greatly influence how others perceive and respond to them. Develop a persuasive communication style that focuses on clarity, brevity, and relevance. Tailor your message to your audience by highlighting the benefits and value your goals can bring to your organization.

This will attract employers and inspire them to see your potential.

4. Use Effective Storytelling Techniques: Storytelling is a powerful tool for engaging and inspiring others. Create compelling stories that illustrate your journey, struggles, and triumphs. Use storytelling techniques to show how your goals align with the organization and how you can contribute to its success. This approach will captivate the recruiter and leave a lasting impression.

5. Use Visual Aids and Technologies: In today's digital age, technology and visual aids can increase the impact of your communication. Use tools like presentations, infographics, and videos to visually communicate your vision and goals. Use technology platforms to build an online presence that showcases your expertise and accomplishments. This combination of visual elements and technology will make your message more memorable and persuasive.

6. Active listening and feedback: Effective

communication is a two-way street. Practice active listening to understand the employer's views and expectations. Seek feedback to gauge how well your vision and goals resonate with others. This feedback loop allows you to refine your communication approach and ensure that it meets the needs of potential employers.

Communicating vision and goals is an important aspect of professional success. By creating a compelling vision, aligning goals with organizational goals, developing a persuasive communication style, using storytelling techniques, using technology and visual aids, and By practicing active listening, you can effectively communicate your aspirations to potential employers. Remember, effective communication isn't just about conveying information; it's about inspiring and engaging others. So improve your communication skills, express your vision and open the door to a future full of possibilities.

Understanding the Purpose and Types of Behavioral Questions

In a competitive job market, it is important for candidates to prepare well for the interview. One of the most common interview questions that often surprise candidates is the behavioral question. These questions are asked to see how you acted in the past and what you learned from those experiences. This helps us guess how you might do in the future. In this chapter, we'll dive into the goals and types of behavioral questions, equipping candidates with the knowledge they need to succeed in an interview.

Purpose of behavioral questions: Behavioral questions are designed to assess a candidate's ability to respond to real-life work situations. They give employers insight into how candidates have handled certain situations in the past, allowing them to predict how they might handle similar situations in the future. By asking behavioral questions, employers can assess a candidate's skills, problem-solving abilities, communication style, teamwork, and other important qualities.

Types of Behavioral Question

1. Situation question: These questions ask candidates to describe a specific situation they encountered at work. For instance, "can you think of a time when it was difficult for you to finish your work on time?" Candidates should tell a story about a time when something happened. They should explain what was going on, what they were doing, what problems they faced, and what they did to fix the problems.

2. Action-based questions: Action-based questions focus on the candidate's actions and decision-making process in a given situation. Example: "Describe a condition where you had to

make a difficult choice. How did you feel?" Candidates should elaborate on their proficiency in making well-informed decisions.

They should explain what things they thought about when making their decision and why they chose to do what they did.

3. Question based on results: Performance-based questions are used to assess candidate performance. Example: "Share a situation where you resolved a disagreement in your team. What was the outcome?" Job seekers should highlight how they have made a good impact in the situation. This could include things like improving on how the team works together, getting more work done, or making customers happier.

4. Group work questions: Teamwork is an important aspect of most jobs. Employers often ask questions to gauge a candidate's ability to work effectively with others. "As an example, describe a scenario where you encountered a challenging team member and elaborate on your approach in handling the situation." Job applicants should emphasize the ability to resolve conflicts, communicate effectively, and develop

positive working relationships.

5. Guiding questions: Leadership qualities are appreciated in many positions. Candidates may be asked to provide examples of situations in which they have demonstrated leadership skills. For example: "Tell us about a situation where you had to take control of a project or a team. How have you encouraged and advised others? Candidates should emphasize the ability to inspire and influence others, delegate tasks, and achieve successful results.

Behavioral questions are an integral part of the interview process, allowing employers to assess a candidate's past behavior and predict future performance. By understanding the purpose and types of behavioral questions, candidates can effectively prepare their answers, demonstrating their skills, experience, and suitability for the role. Be sure to include specific and detailed examples that highlight your actions, decision-making processes, and positive outcomes. With careful preparation and practice, you'll be able to tackle behavioral issues with confidence and increase your chances of landing your dream job. Good luck!

Below is a selection of common behavioral questions, as well as short sample answers. Remember that your answer should be specific, concise, and relevant to the question posed. Tailor these answers to your experience and track record:

1. Tell me about a situation where you had to deal with a difficult colleague.

Answer: At a previous job, I met a colleague who repeatedly failed to meet deadlines. I scheduled a meeting to discuss the issue, express my concerns, and offer assistance. Together, we developed a plan to improve their time management skills, which leads to better collaboration and on-time completion of the project.

2. Describe a situation where you had to resolve a conflict in your team.

Answer: In a group project, two team members

have conflicting opinions. I held an open discussion where everyone could express their views. Through active listening and mediation, we reached a compromise that embraced both perspectives, leading to a successful project outcome.

3. Can you give an example of a situation where you demonstrated good problem-solving skills?

Answer: In my previous role, we faced sudden budget cuts. To address this, I conducted a thorough analysis of our costs, identified areas for savings, and suggested alternatives. My proactive approach reduced the costs by 20% while maintaining productivity.

4. Describe a situation in which you had to adapt to significant changes in the workplace.

Answer: During my previous transition to enterprise-wide software, I learned the importance of adapting quickly. I actively participated in training, sought expert advice, and offered to support colleagues who were struggling with change. My adaptability and willingness to help others helped minimize disruption and ensure a smooth transition.

5. Tell me about a situation where you had to deal with multiple priorities at once.

Answer: During a particularly busy time, I received several urgent requests from various departments. To effectively manage my workload, I prioritized tasks based on their time and importance. I also liaise with stakeholders to manage expectations and ensure all projects are delivered on time.

6. Can you give an example of a time when you demonstrated outstanding leadership skills?

Answer: In my previous role as team leader, I initiated a mentoring program to help foster professional growth within the team. By combining experienced staff with junior members, we created a supportive environment that fosters knowledge sharing, skill development and overall team performance.

7. Describe a situation where you had to take responsibility for a mistake and correct it.

Answer: I made a mistake on a previous project that resulted in a delayed delivery. I immediately reported it to my superiors took responsibility for the mistake and came up with a solution. By working overtime and coordinating with the team, we were able to minimize delays and complete the project successfully.

8. Tell me about a situation where you had to deal with a difficult customer.

Answer: In my previous role as a customer service representative, I met with a customer who was unhappy with our product. I actively listen to their concerns, empathize with their frustrations, and offer solutions that meet their needs. By providing exceptional service, I turned their negative experience into a positive, keeping them loyal.

9. Illustrate a scenario in which you were compelled to perform under demanding circumstances in order to meet a challenging time constraint.

Answer: At my previous job, we had a spike in workload that required tight deadlines. I held a team meeting to assign tasks, set clear priorities, and set a timeline. Thanks to efficient time management, cooperation and focus, we were able to complete the project ahead of schedule.

10. Can you tell us about a situation where you had to deal with a difficult team member?

Answer: On a previous project, I had a team member who was constantly late for deadlines and was not held accountable. I approached him privately to express my concerns and offer assistance. By providing clear expectations, regular reviews, and constructive feedback, we were able to improve their performance, leading to better team dynamics and successful project completion.

11. Describe a situation where you had to resolve a dispute with a colleague.

Answer: During a team meeting, my colleague and I disagreed on the best approach for the project. Instead of allowing differences to escalate, I actively listen to their views, ask clarifying questions, and find common ground. Through open communication and compromise, we have found a common solution that combines both of our ideas.

12. Tell me about a situation when you needed to learn a new skill quickly.

Answer: In my previous position, I was assigned a project that required knowledge of a programming language that I did not know. Realizing the importance of this skill, I signed up for an online course, spent some extra time practicing, and asked for advice from colleagues. Thanks to my own dynamism and perseverance, I quickly acquired the necessary skills and successfully completed the project.

13. Can you give an example of a situation where you had to manage a project with limited

resources?

Answer: In my previous role, I was assigned to manage a project with a limited budget. To maximize our resources, I conducted thorough research, negotiated cost-effective solutions with suppliers, and devised efficient processes. By prioritizing and optimizing available resources, we achieved the project goals within the allotted budget.

14. Describe a situation where you had to resolve conflicts between team members.

Answer: In the previous band, the two members had disagreements that affected the band's morale. I scheduled a meeting with both of them, allowing them to express their concerns openly. Through active listening, empathy, and facilitating constructive dialogue, we arrived at a solution that restored harmony within the team and increased overall productivity.

15. Tell me about a time when you experienced a big failure or failure.

Answer: In a previous project, we had a major failure due to a technical error. Instead of wallowing in failure, I took immediate action to identify the root cause, develop a resolution plan, and communicate transparently with stakeholders. Showing a sense of responsibility and resilience, we rose from failure and successfully completed the project.

16. Describe a situation when you had to give constructive feedback to a colleague.
Answer: In my previous role, I noticed that a colleague's presentation skills needed improvement. I reached out to him privately, highlighting his strengths and making specific suggestions for improvement. By providing ongoing support, resources, and feedback, their presentation skills have improved, resulting in more effective and engaging presentations.

17. Can you give an example of a situation where you had to professionally deal with a stressful situation?
Answer: In my previous role, I was responsible for managing an unexpected technical failure event. Despite the pressure, I remained calm, openly communicated with stakeholders about the

situation, and worked closely with the technical team to find a solution quickly. Demonstrating professionalism and problem-solving skills, we saved the event and maintained a positive reputation.

18. Tell me about a situation where you faced ambiguity or uncertainty in a project.
Answer: In the previous project, scope and requirements kept changing. To accommodate the uncertainty, I actively communicated with stakeholders to clarify expectations and priorities. I have also developed a flexible project plan that is regularly reviewed and adjusted as needed, ensuring successful completion of the project despite uncertainty.

19. Describe a situation where you had to convince others to accept your idea or approach.
Answer: In my previous role, I proposed a new marketing strategy to increase customer engagement. To convince my team, I conducted research, gathered data, and put together a compelling presentation that highlighted potential benefits and results. By effectively communicating the value of the idea and solving

the problem, I gained their support and the strategy was successfully implemented.

20. Can you tell us about a situation where you had to work with an unhappy customer or customers?
Answer: In my previous role as a sales representative, I encountered unhappy customers and received defective products. I actively listen to their concerns, sympathize with their frustrations, and take immediate action to resolve the issue. By offering an alternative product and providing exceptional customer service, I turned their negative experience into a positive, ensuring their satisfaction.

21. Describe a situation where you had to manage a project with conflicting priorities.
Answer: In my previous position, I was assigned several projects with overlapping deadlines. I prioritized tasks by assessing their importance and impact on the overall goals. I communicated with stakeholders, set realistic expectations, and effectively delegated responsibilities. Thanks to effective time management and teamwork, I

completed all the projects on time.

22. Tell me about a situation where you had to adapt your communication style to communicate effectively with different audiences.
Answer: In my previous role, I had to present a complex technical concept to a non-technical audience. To ensure ease of understanding, I simplified the information, used relevant examples, and avoided jargon. By adapting my communication style, I was able to get the message across and the audience grasps the concept, leading to productive discussions and informed decision making.

23. Can you give an example of a situation where you had to deal with a limited budget without compromising on quality?
Answer: In the previous project, we had a limited budget but required high quality. I researched possible alternatives, negotiated discounts with suppliers, and optimally allocated resources. By carefully monitoring costs and making strategic decisions, we maintained quality standards without going over budget.

24. Describe a situation when you had to take the initiative to solve a serious problem.
Answer: In a previous role, our team encountered a serious problem that put the project at risk. Recognizing the urgency, I took the lead in coordinating efforts, conducting root cause analysis, and implementing corrective actions. By mobilizing resources, facilitating cooperation and keeping stakeholders informed, we had successfully resolved this issue and kept the project on schedule.

25. Tell me about a situation where you needed to quickly learn a new software or technology.
Answer: In the previous post, we implemented a new CRM system. To quickly adapt, I actively sought out learning opportunities, researched online resources, and practiced using the software a lot. By spending more time learning and testing the system, I became proficient, ensuring a smooth transition for the team and maximizing the benefits of the system.

26. Describe a situation where you had to manage

complex workloads while maintaining quality.
Answer: In my previous position, I had a period of increased workload due to few co-workers. To maintain quality, I prioritized tasks, streamlined processes, and delegated responsibilities where necessary. Thanks to good organization, effective time management and effective communication with the team, we managed to meet deadlines without compromising on quality.

27. Can you tell about a time when you had to overcome resistance to change?
Answer: At the old location, our division underwent a significant restructuring. Some team members were resistant to change and hesitant to adapt. I held team meetings to address issues, clearly communicated the reasons for the change, and emphasize the benefits to individuals and organizations. By facilitating open dialogue and providing support, we successfully transformed and embraced the change.

Be sure to tailor your answers to your experience and achievements. Use the STAR method (situation, task, action, and outcome) to structure your answer and give specific examples. Practice answering these questions to ensure that you can showcase your skills and abilities during the interview.

Here are some behavioral interview questions:

1. Tell me about a time when you had to work as a team to achieve a goal.
2. Describe a situation where you had to deal with a difficult customer or customers.
3. Can you give an example of a situation where you had to resolve conflict in a group?
4. Describe a situation in which you had to adapt to significant changes in the workplace.
5. Tell me about a situation where you had to deal with multiple priorities at once.
6. Can you give an example of a time when you demonstrated outstanding leadership skills?
7. Describe a situation where you had to take responsibility for mistake and correct it.
8. Tell me about a time when you experienced a major setback or setback.

9. Describe a situation when you had to give constructive feedback to a colleague.
10. Can you give an example of a situation where you had to professionally handle a stressful situation?
11. Tell me about a situation where you had to meet a tight deadline under pressure.
12. Describe a situation where you had to convince others to accept your idea or approach.
13. Can you tell us about a situation where you had to work with an unhappy customer or the customers?
14. Describe a situation where you had to manage a project with limited resources.
15. Tell me about a situation when you needed to learn a new skill quickly.
16. Can you give an example of a situation where you had to deal with a difficult team member?
17. Describe a situation when you had to resolve disputes with a colleague.
18. Tell me about a situation where you faced ambiguity or uncertainty in a project.
19. Describe a situation where you had to manage a project with conflicting priorities.
20. Can you give an example of a situation where

you had to adapt your communication style to different audiences?

21. Tell me about a situation where you had to deal with a limited budget without compromising on quality.

22. Describe a situation when you had to take the initiative to solve a serious problem.

23. Can you tell me about a situation where you had to quickly learn new software or technology?

24. Describe a situation where you had to do a large amount of work while maintaining quality.

25. Tell me about a time when you had to overcome resistance to change.

26. Can you give an example of a situation where you had to mentor or train a colleague?

27. Describe a situation where you had to make a difficult decision with limited information.

28. Tell me about a situation where you had to manage a project with a virtual or remote team.

29. Describe a situation where you had to balance the needs of multiple stakeholders.

30. Can you tell us how long it took you to deal with a sensitive or confidential matter?

31. Tell me about a situation where you had to motivate and inspire a team.

32. Describe a situation where you had to deal with a difficult leader or manager.

33. Can you give an example of a situation where you had to deal with a crisis or emergency?

34. Describe a situation where you had to undertake a process or efficiency improvement initiative.

35. Tell me about a situation where you had to collaborate with colleagues from different departments or groups.

36. Can you give an example of a situation where you had to resolve conflicting priorities in multiple projects?

37. Describe a situation where you had to influence and negotiate with others to achieve desired results.

38. Tell me about a situation where you had to adapt your leadership style to different team members.

39. Describe a situation when you had difficulty reviewing or evaluating work.

40. Can you give an example of a situation where you had to deal with major organizational changes?

41. Tell me about a situation where you had to

create and implement a new process or procedure.

42. Describe a situation where you had to resolve an escalated customer complaint.

43. Can you tell us about a situation where you had to manage a project with a limited time frame?

44. Describe a situation where you had to work with a team member who was consistently underperforming.

45. Tell me about a situation where you had to manage a project with different groups of people.

46. Can you give an example of a situation where you had to deal with a situation with ethical considerations?

47. Describe a situation where you had to make a difficult decision with lasting consequences.

48. Tell me about a situation where you had to manage a project with changing requirements.

49. Describe a situation where you handled a buyer or customer who refused to change.

50. Can you tell us about a time when you had to deal with a situation where resources were limited?

51. Tell me about a situation where you handled a

team member who resisted feedback or coaching.

52. Describe a situation where you had to deal with a difficult seller or supplier.

53. Can you give an example of a situation where you had to manage a project with a geographically dispersed team?

54. Tell me about a period where you had to deal with a situation there was no clear direction or guidance.

55. Describe a time when you had to work with a team member who did not meet deadlines or quality standards.

56. Can you tell us about a time when you had to deal with a situation where there were not enough resources or support.

57. Tell me about a situation you had to deal with when communication was interrupted.

58. Describe a situation in which you handled a buyer or customer with unrealistic expectations.

59. Can you give an example of a situation where you had to manage a project with a conflict of interest among stakeholders?

60. Tell me about a situation where you had to deal with a lack of cooperation or teamwork.

61. Describe a situation where you had to deal

with a team member who resisted change or new ideas.

62. Can you tell me about a time where you faced a situation there was no accountability or responsibility?

63. Tell me about a situation where you had to deal with a situation of lack of trust or lack of transparency.

64. Describe a situation where you had to deal with an upset or angry customer.

65. Can you give an example of a situation where you had to manage a project on a tight budget?

66. Tell me about a situation where you had to deal with a situation that lacked clarity or direction.

67. Describe a situation where you had to work with a team member who was not open to feedback or suggestions.

68. Can you tell me about a situation where you had to deal with a situation where you lacked motivation or morale?

69. Describe a situation where you had to deal with a team member who resisted cooperation or teamwork.

70. Can you give an example of a situation where

you had to manage a project with limited support from senior management?

71. Tell me about a time when you had to deal with a situation that lacked innovation or creativity.

72. Tell me about a situation where you had to deal with a situation of lack of trust or lack of transparency.

Remember that during a behavioral interview, it's important to give specific examples from your experience to demonstrate your skills, abilities, and approaches to different situations in the workplace. Good luck with your interview preparation!

Preparing for and Answering Behavioral Questions

It is essential that job seekers are thoroughly prepared at every stage of the hiring process. One of the most important aspects that often surprise candidates is the behavioral interview, where the employer assesses how the candidate has handled certain situations in the past. This part of the book aims to provide job seekers with practical tips and strategies for preparing and answering behavioral questions effectively, ensuring they leave a lasting impression on potential employers.

Understanding behavior problems: Behavioral questions are designed to assess a candidate's past behavior as an indicator of future performance. These questions often begin with phrases like "Tell me about a time when..." or "Give me an example of..." and ask the candidate to give specific examples. In which they have demonstrated certain skills or characteristics. By sharing real stories, candidates can demonstrate their skills and suitability for the role.

1. Research job requirements: Before going for an

interview, it is very important to thoroughly research the job description and identify the key skills and qualities the employer is looking for. Analyze job requirements and make a list of the most relevant skills, experience, and achievements for the position. This will help you anticipate the types of behavioral questions you might be asked.

2. Definition of STAR examples: The STAR (situation, task, action, and outcome) method is an effective framework for structuring responses to behavioral questions. Take the time to memorize and jot down specific examples from your experience that highlight your skills and competencies. For each example, describe the situation, the challenges you faced, the actions you took, and the positive results you achieved.

3. Practice, practice, practice: Practice is the key to mastering behavior problems. Practice your STAR examples, making sure you can express them confidently and succinctly. Practice with friends or family members and even record answers to questions to gauge your performance and identify areas for improvement. The more

you practice, the more comfortable and prepared you will feel during the interview.

4. Customize your answer: While it's important to prepare standardized STAR examples, it's equally important to tailor your answers to the specific job and company you're interviewing for. Highlight aspects of your experience that are directly related to the skills and qualities the employer is asking for. This setting shows your genuine interest and suitability for the role.

5. Highlight transferable skills: Even if you don't have direct experience in a particular field, focus on transferable skills that are applicable to the role. Mark moments when you successfully adapted to new situations, learned quickly, or demonstrated resilience and problem-solving skills. This shows your ability to transfer your skills and adapt to new challenges.

6. Be honest and brief: Be honest and sincere when answering behavioral questions. Employers value honest answers and can easily tell when candidates are exaggerating or giving generic

answers. Be brief and stick to key details to make your answer clear and easy to understand.

7. Demonstrate self-awareness and development: In addition to demonstrating one's strengths, it is equally important to demonstrate self-awareness and the ability to learn from experience. Be prepared to talk about situations in which you struggled or made mistakes, and explained how you have grown and become better. This emphasizes your willingness to learn and adapt to qualities that are highly valued by employers.

Addressing behavior issues is an important step in the job search process. By carefully preparing, practicing, and tailoring your answers, you'll be able to confidently present your skills, experience, and qualities to potential employers. Make sure your answers are authentic, short, and sincere, and use the STAR method to structure your answers effectively. With these strategies in hand, you can approach any behavioral interview with confidence and increase your chances of landing your dream job.

Common Mistake to Avoid When Answering Behavioral Questions

In competitive job market, employers increasingly rely on behavioral questions to assess a candidate's skills, experience, and suitability for the job. These questions require candidates to provide specific examples from their past experiences to demonstrate their problem-solving abilities and skills. However, many candidates fall into the typical trap of answering behavioral questions, which reduces their chances of landing their dream job. In this part of the book, we'll look at some of these mistakes and provide practical tips to help job seekers avoid them.

1. Unprepared: One of the most common mistakes job seekers make is not being prepared enough to answer behavioral questions. Many people assume that they can only rely on past experience without realizing the importance of

tailoring their responses to the specific requirements of the job. To avoid this, **_candidates should thoroughly research the company and the position they are applying for._** Understanding the values, goals and desired competencies of the organization will allow candidates to tailor their response to the company's expectations.

2. Give an incomplete or unclear answer: When answering behavioral questions, it's important to keep your answers clear and concise. Many candidates make the mistake of giving incomplete or unclear answers, leaving the interviewer's questions unanswered. To avoid this, candidates should use the STAR (Situation, Task, Action, and Result) method to structure their responses. By giving specific examples and highlighting the impact of their actions, candidates can effectively showcase their skills and experience.

3. Focus on personal achievement: Another common mistake is to focus only on personal achievement when answering behavioral questions. **_While emphasizing individual contribution is important, emphasizing_**

teamwork and collaboration is equally important. Employers value candidates who can work well with others and contribute to a positive work environment. Candidates must demonstrate the ability to collaborate, delegate tasks, and communicate effectively within a team.

4. Ignore emphasizing lessons learned: Behavioral questions are often designed to assess a candidate's ability to learn from previous experiences. Many job seekers do not pay enough attention to the valuable lessons they have learned from difficult situations. To avoid this mistake, candidates should discuss how they have grown and developed through their experience. By demonstrating a growth mindset and a willingness to learn from their mistakes, candidates can demonstrate adaptability and resilience.

5. Excessive use of jargon or technical language: Using too much jargon or technical language is a common mistake that can be overlooked by interviewers unfamiliar with certain terms. Job seekers should be aware that interviewers may

come from a variety of backgrounds and may not have the same technical expertise. It is essential to communicate clearly and precisely, avoiding complicated jargon. Candidates should focus on explaining their experience and skills in a way that is understandable to a wide audience.

6. No question: At the end of the interview, candidates often have the opportunity to ask questions. Not using this feature is a common mistake that can leave a negative impression on the interviewer. Thoughtful and relevant questions not only show genuine interest but also allow the candidate to gather more information about the position and the company. ***It is advisable to prepare some questions in advance so as not to miss this opportunity.***

7. Rambling or Going Off-Topic: Providing long-winded answers that stray from the original question can make it challenging for interviewers to follow the applicant's thought process.

8. Being Too Negative or Critical: Speaking

negatively about past employers or experiences can raise concerns about the candidate's attitude and professionalism.

9. Lack of Confidence: Displaying a lack of confidence in one's abilities can give the impression of insecurity and uncertainty.

10. Not Demonstrating Problem-Solving Skills: Failing to provide concrete examples of how the candidate has overcome challenges can make it difficult for interviewers to assess your problem-solving abilities.

11. Lack of Self-Awareness: Not being aware of one's strengths and weaknesses can hinder the ability to bring relevant and accurate examples of experiences.

12. Not Showing Enthusiasm: Failing to convey genuine excitement and passion for the role can make the candidate appear disinterested or unmotivated.

13. Too General: Providing vague or generic

responses without specific examples can make it challenging for interviewers to assess the candidate's abilities.

14. Not Admitting Mistakes: Failing to acknowledge and take responsibility for past mistakes can raise concerns about accountability and integrity.

15. Lack of Preparation for Behavioral Questions: Not anticipating and practicing responses to common behavioral questions can lead to unstructured and ineffective answers.

16. Poor Body Language: Displaying negative body language, such as slouching or avoiding eye contact, can give the impression of disengagement or lack of confidence.

17. Not Listening Carefully: **Failing to actively listen to the interviewer's question can result in providing irrelevant or off-topic answers.**

18. Exaggerating or Lying: *Providing false information or exaggerating achievements can damage credibility and trust.*

19. Not Following the STAR Method: Neglecting to structure answers using the STAR method (Situation, Task, Action, and Result) can result in disorganized and unclear responses.

20. Not Asking Questions: Failing to ask thoughtful and relevant questions at the end of the interview can give the impression of disinterest or lack of curiosity.

21. Lack of Clarity in Communication: Not articulating thoughts and experiences clearly can lead to confusion and misinterpretation.

22. Being Too Humble: While humility is important, downplaying achievements excessively can make it difficult for interviewers to gauge the candidate's capabilities.

23. Not Demonstrating Adaptability: Failing to showcase the ability to adapt to new situations or changes in the workplace can raise concerns about flexibility.

24. Overemphasizing Personal Preferences:

Placing too much emphasis on personal preferences rather than aligning with the company's values and goals can give the impression of being self-centered.

25. Not Highlighting Leadership Skills: Neglecting to showcase leadership abilities, such as delegation, decision-making, and motivating others, can be a missed opportunity for candidates aiming for managerial roles.

26. Lack of Emotional Intelligence: Not demonstrating empathy, self-awareness, and the ability to manage emotions effectively can raise concerns about the candidate's interpersonal skills.

27. Not Providing Quantifiable Results: Failing to quantify achievements with specific numbers or metrics can make it challenging for interviewers to gauge the impact of the candidate's actions.

28. Being Too Rigid: Displaying an unwillingness to adapt or consider alternative approaches can raise concerns about the candidate's ability to

work in a dynamic environment.

29. Lack of Cultural Fit: Not showcasing an understanding of the company's culture and values can make it difficult for interviewers to assess whether the candidate would be a good fit within the organization.

30. Not Demonstrating Initiative: Failing to provide examples of taking initiative, going above and beyond, or seeking opportunities for growth can give the impression of being passive or lacking motivation.

32. Lack of Industry Knowledge: Failing to demonstrate a solid understanding of the industry and its trends can make it challenging for interviewers to assess the candidate's suitability for the role.

33. Not Showing Interest in Professional Development: Neglecting to discuss ongoing efforts to enhance skills and knowledge can raise concerns about the candidate's commitment to growth.

34. Poor Time Management: Not providing examples of effective time management and prioritization skills can raise concerns about the candidate's ability to meet deadlines and handle multiple tasks.

35. Not Demonstrating Customer Focus: For customer-facing roles, not highlighting a customer-centric mindset and the ability to handle customer inquiries or complaints can be a significant drawback.

36. Lack of Confidence in Handling Conflict: Failing to showcase the ability to navigate and resolve conflicts can raise concerns about the candidate's interpersonal and problem-solving skills.

37. Not Demonstrating Attention to Detail: For roles that require meticulousness, not highlighting attention to detail and accuracy can make it challenging for interviewers to assess the candidate's suitability.

38. Lack of Professionalism: Displaying

unprofessional behavior, such as arriving late, using inappropriate language, or lacking proper attire, can create a negative impression.

39. Not Demonstrating Continuous Learning: Failing to showcase a commitment to ongoing learning and professional development can raise concerns about the candidate's ability to adapt to new technologies and industry advancements.

40. Lack of Enthusiasm for the Company: Not conveying genuine interest and enthusiasm for the company and its mission can make it difficult for interviewers to gauge the candidate's level of commitment.

41. Overlooking Non-Verbal Communication: Not paying attention to non-verbal cues, such as maintaining eye contact and using appropriate gestures, can impact the overall impression a candidate leaves on interviewers.

42. Not Providing Specific Examples: Failing to provide specific instances and examples from experiences can make it challenging

for interviewers to assess the candidate's skills and abilities.

43. Inability to Handle Stress: Not highlighting the ability to remain calm and composed under pressure can raise concerns about the candidate's resilience and ability to handle challenging situations.

44. Lack of Research on the Interviewer: Failing to research the interviewer's background and role within the company can miss an opportunity to establish rapport and ask targeted questions.

45. Not Demonstrating Problem Prevention: Focusing solely on problem-solving without showcasing the ability to identify and prevent issues before they arise can be a missed opportunity to highlight proactive skills.

46. Overemphasizing Salary and Benefits: *Placing excessive emphasis on salary and benefits during the interview process can give the impression of being solely motivated by monetary rewards.*

47. Not Demonstrating Initiative in Learning about the Company: Failing to showcase efforts made to learn about the company beyond surface-level information can indicate a lack of genuine interest.

48. Lack of Adaptability to Remote Work: In the current work landscape, not highlighting the ability to work effectively remotely can hinder opportunities for candidates seeking remote or hybrid roles.

49. Not Demonstrating Respect for Diversity and Inclusion: Failing to showcase an understanding and appreciation for diversity and inclusion can raise concerns about the candidate's ability to work in diverse teams.

50. Lack of Follow-Up: Neglecting to send a thank-you note or follow-up email after the interview can give the impression of disinterest or lack of professionalism.

Conclusion

Possessing technical expertise alone is no longer sufficient to secure your dream job. Employers are prioritizing candidates with strong soft skills and the ability to excel in behavioral-based interviews. This comprehensive manual serves as a valuable resource for job seekers, providing guidance on mastering these essential skills and techniques. By understanding the importance of **soft skills** and preparing for behavioral-based interviews, you can unleash your full career power and stand out from the competition.

The Power of Soft Skills:
Soft skills, such as communication, teamwork, flexibility, and problem-solving, are crucial for success in any professional field. This manual emphasizes the significance of developing and showcasing these skills to potential employers. By focusing on areas like emotional intelligence, leadership, and conflict resolution, you can enhance your chances of landing your desired job. The manual offers practical tips and exercises to

help you improve these skills and demonstrate your value to employers.

Behavioral-Based Interview Questions: Behavioral-based interviews have become increasingly popular among hiring managers. These interviews require candidates to provide specific examples of experiences that highlight their abilities and behaviors in various work-related situations. This guide provides a comprehensive model for preparing and acing such interviews. It offers a step-by-step approach to understanding the STAR (Situation, Task, Action, Result) technique, enabling you to effectively structure your responses and impress interviewers.

Key Takeaways:
Throughout this manual, job seekers will find a wealth of valuable insights and tools to enhance their career prospects. By mastering soft skills, you can differentiate yourself from other candidates and demonstrate your potential for success. The manual also equips you with the knowledge, **jargons to avoid** and techniques

needed to excel in behavioral-based interviews, ensuring you leave a lasting impression on hiring managers.

Unleashing your full career potential requires a well-rounded skill set that extends beyond technical expertise. By mastering the soft skills that employers seek and acing behavioral-based interviews, you can position yourself as an exceptional candidate in today's competitive job market. ***This comprehensive manual serves as your go-to resource,*** providing valuable guidance and practical exercises to help you develop and showcase your skills effectively. Embrace the opportunities presented by this manual, and embark on a journey towards a successful and fulfilling career. ***Remember, your potential is limitless; all you need is the right knowledge and strategies to unlock it.***

Recap of Key Points

in this book, we covered several key points to help job seekers unleash their full career potential by mastering soft skills and acing behavioral-based interview questions. Here is a recap of the key points examined.

1. Importance of Soft Skills: We emphasized that possessing technical expertise is no longer enough in today's job market. Soft skills, such as communication, teamwork, adaptability, and problem-solving, are crucial for success.

2. Developing Soft Skills: The manual provides practical tips and exercises to help job seekers improve their soft skills. Areas like emotional intelligence, leadership, and conflict resolution are highlighted as essential skills to develop.

3. Showcasing Soft Skills: We discussed the significance of showcasing soft skills to potential employers. By highlighting specific examples and accomplishments, job seekers can demonstrate

their value and differentiate themselves from other applicants.

4. Behavioral-Based Interviews: We introduced the concept of behavioral-based interviews, which are increasingly popular among hiring managers. These interviews require candidates to provide specific examples of past experiences to showcase their abilities and behaviors.

5. The STAR Technique: We provided a comprehensive model for preparing and acing behavioral-based interviews using the STAR technique (Situation, Task, Action, and Result). This approach helps to structure responses and impress interviewers.

6. Practical Guidance: Throughout the book, we offered practical guidance and exercises to help job seekers enhance their soft skills and prepare for behavioral-based interviews. These tools are designed to equip candidates with the knowledge and strategies needed to succeed.

7. Unleashing Career Potential: The ultimate goal

of this book is to help job seekers unleash their full career potential. By mastering soft skills and excelling in behavioral-based interviews, candidates can position themselves as exceptional candidates and increase their chances of securing their desired jobs.

By implementing the insights and strategies provided in this book, job seekers can confidently navigate the job market, stand out from the competition, and unlock their full career potential.

Mastering Soft Skill for Job Seekers: A Comprehensive Guide to Succeeding in Interviews and the Workplace

Technical skills alone are no longer sufficient. Employers are increasingly placing emphasis on soft skills, which are essential for effective communication, collaboration, and problem-solving. This article, based on the enlightening book "Unlocking Career Opportunities: The Power of Soft Skills in Job Searching," provides job seekers with practical insights on how to apply and master soft skills in interviews and the workplace, helping them stand out and succeed in their professional endeavors.

Understanding Soft Skills:
Soft skills encompass a broad range of personal attributes and interpersonal abilities that enable individuals to work well with others. These skills include communication, adaptability, leadership, teamwork, problem-solving, and emotional

intelligence. Recognizing the significance of these skills is the first step towards developing and showcasing them effectively.

Preparing for Job Interviews:
1. Research the Company: Gain a thorough understanding of the company's values, culture, and goals to align your responses and demonstrate your fit.

2. Behavioral-Based Questions: Practice answering questions that assess your soft skills by providing specific examples from experiences that highlight your abilities.
3. Highlight Adaptability: Emphasize instances where you successfully adapted to change or overcame challenges, showcasing your ability to thrive in dynamic environments.

Applying Soft Skills in the Workplace:
1. Effective Communication: Actively listen, articulate ideas clearly, and show empathy towards colleagues, fostering a positive and collaborative work environment.
2. Leadership and Teamwork: Demonstrate

initiative, inspire others, and work well with colleagues to achieve common goals, showcasing your leadership and teamwork abilities.

3. Problem-Solving and Critical Thinking: Analyze situations objectively, identify potential solutions, and make informed decisions, displaying your ability to think critically and find effective solutions.

4. Conflict Resolution: Show your ability to manage conflicts and resolve disagreements professionally and constructively. This includes active listening, understanding different viewpoints, seeking common ground, and finding win-win solutions that satisfy all parties involved.

Acknowledgement

I would like to express my deepest gratitude and appreciation to all the individuals who have contributed to the creation of "Unlocking Career Opportunities: The Power of Soft Skills in Job Searching." Your support and dedication have been invaluable in bringing this project to fruition.

First and foremost, I would like to acknowledge all the **job hunters around the globe** who have shared their experiences and insights. Your stories have provided the foundation for this book, and your determination and resilience in navigating the job market have been truly inspiring.

I would also like to extend my gratitude to the various platforms that have played a significant role in connecting job seekers with potential employers. Special thanks to platforms such as LinkedIn, Indeed, Glassdoor, and CareerBuilder, among many others. Your commitment to providing a space for job seekers to showcase their skills and connect with employment opportunities has been instrumental in shaping the landscape of job searching.

Additionally, I would like to recognize the countless career coaches and mentors who have dedicated their time and expertise to supporting job seekers. Your guidance and advice have been invaluable in helping individuals develop their soft skills and enhance their chances of success in the job market.

Furthermore, I would like to thank the academic institutions, training centers, and vocational schools that have incorporated soft skills development into their curricula. Your commitment to equipping job seekers with the necessary skills for career advancement has been crucial in bridging the gap between education and employment.

Last but not least, I would like to express my heartfelt appreciation to my colleagues and friends who have provided unwavering support throughout this journey. Your encouragement and feedback have been invaluable in shaping the content and ensuring its relevance to job seekers worldwide.

To all those mentioned and those who have contributed behind the scenes, thank you for your invaluable contributions to "Unlocking Career Opportunities: The Power of Soft Skills in Job Searching." Your dedication to helping job seekers unlock their potential and find fulfilling careers is truly commendable.

I would like to extend a special mention and express my deepest gratitude to the following individuals for their exceptional contributions to the content creation on LinkedIn:

1. Brigette Hyacinth
2. Rachel Mitchell
3. Ravi Narayanan
4. Jandeep Singh
5. Bernie Fussenegger
6. Maria Cecilia Conde
7. Anatoli Ulitrovsky
8. Marlene Foster
9. Patricia Travis
10. Audrey Van Der Lee
11. Derick Mildred
12. Liliana Maruta

13. Angie World
14. Leadership First
15. Muhammad Sajwani
16. Antonio Prescott
17. Henry Edward
18. Tracy Murray
19. Tulsi Soni
20. Mamaliz Liz Franklin
21. Raji Gupta (Lifting others)

Your dedication to creating insightful and valuable content on LinkedIn has not only provided immense value to job seekers but has also helped shape the professional landscape. Your expertise and thought leadership have been instrumental in empowering individuals around the world to unlock their career opportunities.

Once again, I extend my heartfelt appreciation to all of you for your outstanding contributions.

Bonus - Unlock achievements Job interview Jargons to Avoid

1. Synergy:

This term refers to the cooperation and combined efforts of several individuals or groups to achieve a common goal. Instead of using this jargon, job seekers should focus on highlighting their good teamwork and past experience of successful collaboration.

2. Transform model:

This phrase describes a significant change in the way something is perceived or done. Job seekers should avoid using this term and instead explain how they are adapting to changes and adopting new approaches to their work.

3. Creative thinking:

This phrase encourages creative thinking and innovation. Instead of using this jargon, job seekers should provide specific examples of how they approached problems or projects in unique and creative ways.

4. Ripe fruit:

This term refers to opportunities or solutions that are easily achievable or readily available. Job seekers should avoid using this jargon and instead focus the discussion on the ability to identify and prioritize tasks that can yield immediate results.

5. Basic capacity:

This phrase represents unique strengths or abilities that distinguish a person or organization from others. Job seekers should explain their specific skills and expertise that make them the ideal candidate for the position without relying on this jargon.

6. Leverage:

This term means to use resources or advantages to maximize results or outcomes. Job seekers should avoid using this jargon and instead provide specific examples of how they have used their skills and resources effectively in previous roles.

7. Best practice:

This term refers to the most effective or efficient method or approach to achieve a desired result. Job seekers should explain their approach to problem solving and decision making, highlighting their ability to adapt and learn from past experiences.

8. Value added:

This sentence describes additional benefits or improvements provided beyond the basic requirements. Job seekers should focus on how they go beyond their previous role to deliver exceptional results or add additional value to their team or clients.

9. Seamless integration:

This term refers to the harmonious and effective combination of different components or systems. Job seekers should explain their ability to adapt to new environments and work well with diverse teams without relying on this jargon.

10. Breakthrough innovation:

This phrase describes a disruptive or disruptive innovation that dramatically changes an industry or market. Job seekers should avoid using this jargon and instead discuss their ability to adapt to changing industry trends and come up with innovative ideas.

11. Game changer:

This term refers to a person, idea, or development that significantly impacts and changes the course of a situation or industry. Job seekers should focus on demonstrating the ability to make positive and impactful changes to their previous role without relying on this jargon.

12. Optimization:

This term means to improve or enhance efficiency, performance or effectiveness. Job seekers should explain their ability to identify areas for improvement and implement strategies to optimize processes or outcomes.

13. Rationalization:

The term implies simplifying or eliminating unnecessary steps or processes to make something more efficient. Job seekers should provide examples of how they have streamlined their workflow or improved efficiency in their previous roles.

14. ROI (Return on Investment):

This acronym is a measure of the profitability or value derived from an investment. Job seekers should focus their discussion on their ability to deliver measurable results and deliver value to their employer without relying on this jargon.

15. KPIs (Key Performance Indicators):

This acronym refers to a quantifiable metric used to evaluate or measure performance. Job seekers should describe their ability to set and achieve goals, reach them, and deliver results without relying solely on this jargon.

16. Offline use:

This phrase suggests discussing a topic or issue outside the current meeting or conversation. Job seekers should focus on maintaining clear and effective communication during interviews and avoid using this jargon.

17. Drill down:

This expression means to delve deeper into a particular topic or analyze something in more detail. Job seekers should describe their ability to conduct thorough research, analyze data, and provide meaningful insights without resorting to this jargon.

18. Deep dives:

Like "drill down", the term implies thorough and comprehensive investigation or analysis. Job seekers should focus on demonstrating analytical skills and the ability to dig into details when necessary without resorting to this jargon.

19. Service:

The term refers to a tangible or measurable outcome or outcome expected from a project or task. Job seekers should not rely solely on this jargon and should focus on discussing their ability to meet deadlines, deliver quality work, and obtain desired results.

20. On boarding:

This term refers to the process of integrating and training new employees into an organization. Candidates should describe their ability to quickly adapt to new environments and learn new processes and systems without relying solely on this jargon.

21. Growth Hack:

The term refers to innovative and unconventional strategies for companies to grow rapidly. Job seekers should avoid using this jargon and instead focus on discussing their ability to drive growth and achieve goals through strategic thinking and execution.

22. Current Status:

The term describes being at the forefront of innovation or technology. Job seekers should avoid using this jargon and instead provide examples of how they have kept up with industry trends and embraced new technologies and practices.

23. Idea:

The term means idea generation or brainstorming. Job seekers should avoid using this jargon and instead discuss their ability to come up with creative ideas and participate in shared problem solving.

24. Move the needle.

This phrase means to make a big impact or bring about a big change. Job seekers should avoid using this jargon and instead provide examples of how they have made a positive impact or achieved noticeable results in their previous positions.

25. Customer focus:

The term describes a focus on putting the customer at the center of decision-making and strategy. Job seekers should avoid using this jargon and instead talk about their ability to understand and effectively meet customer needs.

26. Thought Leaders:

The term refers to a person who is recognized as an expert or influential person in a particular industry or field. Job seekers should avoid using this jargon and instead focus on using specific examples to showcase their industry knowledge and expertise.

27. Ecosystem:

The term refers to a complex network of interconnected units or components. Candidates should avoid using this jargon and instead provide examples of how they have navigated and collaborated successfully in complex work environments.

28. Monetization:

This term means to generate revenue or profit from something. Job seekers should avoid using this jargon and instead focus on discussing the ability to identify and capitalize on revenue-generating or cost-saving opportunities.

29. Agile:

The term refers to an iterative and flexible approach to project management. Job seekers should avoid using this jargon and instead discuss their ability to adapt to changing priorities, work well in a fast-paced environment, and manage projects effectively.

30. Disruptor:

The term refers to a business or innovation that significantly disrupts an industry. Job seekers should avoid using this jargon and instead focus on discussing the ability to adapt to changing market conditions and drive positive change.

31. Pivot:

This term describes a strategic shift in direction or focus. Job seekers should avoid using this jargon and instead explain how they successfully adapt to changing circumstances or seize new opportunities.

32. Value proposition:

This term refers to the unique value or benefit that a product, service, or individual provides. Job seekers should avoid using this jargon and instead focus on clearly presenting their skills, experience, and how they can bring value to the organization.

33. Scalable:

This term describes the ability of a business or solution to manage growth without significant changes. Job seekers should avoid using this jargon and instead discuss their experience managing development or handling increased responsibilities.

34. Disintermediation:

This term refers to the elimination of intermediaries in the supply chain or distribution process. Job seekers should avoid using this jargon and instead focus the discussion on their ability to streamline processes or improve efficiency.

35. Bleeding - edge:

This term describes being at the forefront of technological innovation. Job seekers should avoid using this jargon and instead provide examples of how they have embraced new technologies or kept up to date with industry trends.

36. Value chain:

This term describes a range of activities that add value to a product or service. Job seekers should avoid using this jargon and instead discuss their experiences optimizing processes or improving the overall value proposition.

37. Disruption:

This term refers to a significant change or disruption affecting an industry or market. Job seekers should avoid using this jargon and instead focus on discussing the ability to adapt to change and produce positive results.

38. Holistic:

This term describes an approach that considers the whole system or context. Job seekers should avoid using this jargon and instead focus on discussing their ability to see the big picture and consider multiple perspectives.

39. Mind share:

This term refers to the level of awareness or attention that a brand or idea requires. Job seekers should avoid using this jargon and instead focus on discussing the ability to effectively communicate ideas and build relationships.

40. Win win:

This term describes a situation where all parties involved benefit. Job seekers should avoid using this jargon and instead provide examples of how they have successfully negotiated or collaborated to achieve a win-win outcome.

41. Blue-sky thinking:

This term refers to thinking without limits or constraints. Job seekers should avoid using this jargon and instead discuss their ability to think creatively and come up with creative solutions.

42. Growth Mindset:

This term describes the belief that abilities and intelligence can be developed through effort and learning. Job seekers should avoid using this jargon and instead focus on discussing their willingness to learn, adapt and meet challenges.

43. Value stream:

This term refers to the steps or processes involved in creating value for the customer. Job seekers should avoid using this jargon and instead discuss their experience optimizing workflows or improving customer experiences.

44. Discreet:

This term describes something that is different. Job seekers should avoid using this jargon and instead focus on providing clear examples of their accomplishments or skills without relying on vague jargon.

45. Actionable:

This term describes something that can be done or done. Job seekers should avoid using this jargon and instead focus the discussion on their ability to come up with practical and proactive solutions.

46. Bandwidth:

This term refers to the capacity or resources available to manage tasks or responsibilities. Job seekers should avoid using this jargon and discuss their ability to effectively manage multiple tasks or projects instead.

47. Best in class:

This term describes being a top performer or leader in a particular field. Job seekers should avoid using this jargon and instead focus the discussion on achieving outstanding results or recognition in their field.

48. Benchmark:

This term refers to a standard or benchmark used for comparison purposes. Job seekers should avoid using this jargon and instead discuss their ability to set and exceed performance goals or industry standards.

49. Big Data:

This term describes large and complex data sets that can be analyzed for better understanding. Job seekers should avoid using this jargon and instead focus on discussing their experience in analyzing and extracting meaningful insights from data.

50. Business Process Reengineering:

This term refers to the redesign of business processes to improve efficiency and effectiveness. Job seekers should avoid using this jargon and instead discuss their experiences streamlining processes or driving operational improvements.

51. Buzzword:

This term refers to an overused buzzword or word or phrase. Job seekers should avoid using buzzwords and instead focus on clear and concise communication.

52. C level:

This term refers to management positions such as CEO, CFO or CTO. Job seekers should avoid using this jargon and instead use specific job titles or describe their experience working with senior management.

53. Change agent:

This term describes a person who promotes and manages change within an organization. Job seekers should avoid using this jargon and instead discuss their experiences leading change initiatives or leading positive transformations.

54. Cloud computing:

This term refers to the provision of computer services over the Internet. Job seekers should avoid using this jargon and instead discuss their experiences using cloud-based technologies or working with remote teams.

55. Core Values:

This term refers to the underlying beliefs or principles that guide an organization. Job seekers should avoid using this jargon and instead discuss their alignment with the company's values and commitment to ethical conduct.

56. Customer journey:

This term describes the process or stages a customer goes through when interacting with a business. Job seekers should avoid using this jargon and instead discuss their experience in understanding client needs and delivering an exceptional experience.

57. Digital transformations:

The term refers to the integration of digital technologies into all aspects of a business. Job seekers should avoid using this jargon and instead discuss their experiences using digital tools or leading digital initiatives.

58. Empowerment:

This term means to give someone authority or power to do something. Job seekers should avoid using this jargon and instead discuss the possibility of delegating responsibility, trusting their team members, and fostering a collaborative work environment.

59. Human capital:

This term refers to the collective skills, knowledge, and abilities of employees in an organization. Job seekers should avoid using this jargon and instead discuss their experience in growing and nurturing talent.

60. Hyper local:

This term describes a concentration on a particular geographic area or community. Job seekers should avoid using this jargon and instead provide examples of their experience in understanding the local market and tailoring strategies accordingly.

61. Impactful:

This term describes something that has a significant impact or influence. Job seekers should avoid using this jargon and instead provide specific examples of their accomplishments and the positive results they have produced.

62. Innovation:

This term refers to the creation or introduction of new ideas, products, or processes. Job seekers should avoid using this jargon and instead discuss their ability to think creatively, embrace change, and foster innovation in their work.

63. Intellectual Property:

The term refers to the legal rights that protect intellectual creations, such as inventions or works of art. Job seekers should avoid using this jargon and instead discuss their experience in managing and protecting intellectual property.

64. Lean Methodology:

The term refers to a systematic approach to eliminating waste and maximizing process value. Job seekers should avoid using this jargon and instead discuss their experience in process improvement or efficiency

65. Machine Learning:

The term refers to the use of algorithms and statistical models to enable computers to learn from data and make predictions. Job seekers should avoid using this jargon and instead discuss their experiences using data-driven insights or working with predictive models.

66. Minimum Viable Product (MVP):

This term refers to the release of a product that is functional enough to satisfy initial customers and gather feedback for future development. Job seekers should avoid using this jargon and instead discuss their experiences launching successful products or projects.

67. Omni-channel:

This term describes a seamless and integrated customer experience across multiple channels or platforms. Job seekers should avoid using this jargon and instead discuss their ability to deliver a consistent and personalized experience across different touch points.

68. Paradigm:

This term refers to a fundamental change in thinking or approach. Job seekers should avoid using this jargon and instead give examples of how they have adapted to new situations or embraced innovative ideas.

69. SaaS (Software as a Service):

The term refers to a software delivery model in which applications are hosted in the cloud and accessed over the Internet. Job seekers should avoid using this jargon and instead discuss their experiences using cloud-based solutions or working with software applications.

70. Stakeholder:

This term refers to individuals or groups that have an interest or influence in a project or organization. Job seekers should avoid using this jargon and instead discuss their experience in managing relationships with various stakeholders and meeting their needs.

71. Total cost of ownership (TCO):

This term refers to the total costs associated with owning and operating a product or solution. Job seekers should avoid using this jargon and instead discuss their ability to analyze costs, make informed decisions, and optimize resources.

72. User Experience (UX):

This term refers to the overall experience of a user when interacting with a product or system. Job seekers should avoid using this jargon and instead discuss their experience designing intuitive and user-friendly experiences.

73. Work-life balance:

This term refers to the balance between work and personal life. Job seekers should avoid using this jargon and instead discuss the ability to manage priorities, stay happy, and achieve harmony between work and personal commitments.

74. Zero-sum game:

This term refers to a situation where one person's gain is precisely offset by another's loss. Job seekers should avoid using this jargon and instead focus on discussing the possibility of creating win-win situations and fostering collaboration.

75. 360 degree feedback:

The term refers to a feedback process that involves the gathering of information from multiple sources, including supervisors, peers, and subordinates. Job seekers should avoid using this jargon and instead discuss their experiences in receiving and providing constructive feedback to enhance their personal and professional growth.

Printed in Great Britain
by Amazon